The President as Leader

❖ ❖ ❖ ❖ ❖ ❖ ❖ ❖ ❖ ❖ ❖ ❖ ❖ ❖ ❖

The President as Leader

APPEALING TO THE BETTER ANGELS OF OUR NATURE

Erwin C. Hargrove

UNIVERSITY PRESS OF KANSAS

BMG 4149-4/1

©1998 by the University Press of Kansas

All rights reserved

Published by the University Press of Kansas (Lawrence, Kansas 66049), which was organized by the Kansas Board of Regents and is operated and funded by Emporia State University, Fort Hays State University, Kansas State University, Pittsburg State University, the University of Kansas, and Wichita State University

Library of Congress Cataloging in Publication Data

Hargrove, Erwin C.

The President as leader : appealing to the better angels of our nature / Erwin C. Hargrove.

p.   cm.

Includes bibliographical references and index.

ISBN 0-7006-0900-8 (cloth : alk. paper)

1. Presidents—United States.   2. Political leadership—United States.   I. Title.

JK516.H275   1998

303.3′4′0973—dc21   98-10515

British Library Cataloguing in Publication Data is available.

Printed in the United States of America

10 9 8 7 6 5 4 3 2 1

The paper used in this publication meets the minimum requirements of the American National Standard for Permanence of Paper for Printed Library Materials Z39.48-1984.

CONTENTS

PREFACE

❖   ❖   ❖

For many years, I have kept a journal of notes about the book on presidential leadership that I would write as the capstone of my career. Each book that I have written on the presidency has served its purpose in depicting the protean character of the office.[1] And I have often wondered whether a final synthesis was possible or even desirable. But gradually my work on political and administrative leadership has appeared to be applicable to the presidency. I have discovered a pattern in my work, looking at it after the fact, that has enabled me to sharpen the journal notes into a plan for a book that would not be a grand synthesis about the presidency but my own personal synthesis.[2] One must find one's own voice, and it is that authenticity that I have sought in this book. This is my statement of the things that I most want to say about presidential leadership. I have felt at times while writing that long digested ideas were tumbling out and that I was the editor as much as the author of this book. As Virginia Woolf wrote of one of her novels, "[E]verything is running of its own accord into the stream."[3]

The themes of this book are the legacy of my work. To be successful, presidents must use skills and embrace goals that are congruent with the historical context. The preeminent skill is discernment of the political possibilities at a given time. Of particular importance is insight into the resources for and constraints on action in the political culture. Presidents must be good at the transactional skills of bargaining and maneuver, but their first task is to "teach reality" to publics and their fellow politicians through rhetoric.[4] Teaching reality involves the explanation of contemporary problems and issues but, at its best, must invoke and interpret the perennial ideals of the American national experience as expressed in the past and present, and as guides for the future.

The central thesis of the book is that ideals about the American experience are the strongest resources that presidents may invoke. In this sense, ideals have utility. But the will to live up to them is moral rather than utilitarian. Democracy is best served if presidents appeal to "the better angels of our nature."[5] This conception of leadership may appear to give short shrift to the calculated strategies and bargains of transactional politics, in which self-interest and representation are paramount. This is not my intention. Nor do I believe that ideals can overcome transactional politics. Even the most idealistic politics incorporates transactional elements into its strategies. But the politics of ideals is the subject of this book.

I make a strong argument on behalf of prudence as a necessary component of the politics of ideals. This may appear to qualify my praise of moral leadership, but it does not. Presidents must be prudent in their discernment of the historical possibilities for action if their idealism is not to become grandiosity. One must be prudent before one can be bold.

Chapter 1 sets the stage for my argument by anchoring the desired attributes of political leaders in Aristotle's insights about statesmanship. His study of comparative constitutions taught him that leaders must base constitutional principles and practice on the special character of the polity they serve. He regarded the practical discernment of what will and will not work in given settings as superior to abstract, deductive maxims and theories. The primary task of statesmen, for Aristotle, was to teach citizens "the spirit of the constitution."

Chapter 2 develops a model with which to analyze, compare, and evaluate political leaders. The concepts of skill in context, discernment, character as a skill, cultural leadership, and teaching reality are set out and their interrelationship is explored. I extract both normative and empirical propositions from the model.

Chapter 3 interprets American political culture, which presidents must understand if they are to discern social possibilities and practice effective politics. Presidents are both empowered and bounded by culture in understandable, if not predictable, ways.

Chapters 4, 5, and 6 analyze and assess the presidencies of Franklin Roosevelt, Lyndon Johnson, and Ronald Reagan according to my model. These three were chosen because, taken together, they illustrate the dimensions of the model, and thus my theoretical search, better than any other combination of presidents. Of course, others should be added in time to test my ideas more fully.

Chapter 7 compares and evaluates the three presidents according to the normative implications of my model. Extending the model, the chapter explores its implications for leadership of democracy, with special attention to skill, character, culture, and teaching reality.

This book is written for the educated reader. I have avoided the terminology of political science whenever possible, but scholars will see my anchoring in the discipline. I do not believe that political scientists require a special language to communicate with one another, nor do I think it desirable. We do not have an applied science like economics. Our work is likely to bear the greatest fruit if it can be understood by a lay public. In studying the presidency, we study ourselves as Americans.

I would like to list my intellectual debts to the scholars who have influenced my thinking over many years. Richard Neustadt and James McGregor Burns have provided a point–counterpoint tension that has spurred me to find a synthesis which incorporates them both. Alexander George is always present as I write about political personality. The broad beams that Louis Hartz and Seymour Martin Lipset have cast on American political culture and the "exceptionalism" of American politics have been of great value. Robert Tucker's exposition of the character of cultural leadership has been incorporated into my work. I am grateful to these intellectual mentors. I owe a great debt to my friend Fred Greenstein, with whom I have discussed the presidency over many years, in many different settings.

Richard Ellis and John Burke read the manuscript in successive drafts for the University Press of Kansas, and their advice was extremely helpful. The book was finished while I was a visiting professor at the University of Leeds, and I thank my friends David Bell, Kevin Theakston, and David Beetham for their patience as an audience. Fred Woodward, the director of the University Press of Kansas, has been a steady source of encouragement. Irene Pavitt is a very astute freelance editor, and I am grateful for her felicity.

The strengths and weaknesses of this book are mine. It will be superseded in time, but that does not bother me. This is the book I wanted to write, and that is sufficient reward.

Finally, I wish to thank my wife, Julie, for simply being there and providing comfort for the pain of authorship.

1

Power and Purpose in Political Leadership

❖ ❖ ❖ ❖ ❖ ❖ ❖ ❖ ❖ ❖ ❖ ❖ ❖ ❖

Abraham Lincoln concluded his first inaugural address with these carefully crafted words: "I am loth to close. We are not enemies but friends.
We must not be enemies. Though passion may have strained, it must not
break our bonds of affection. The mystic chords of memory, stretching
from every battle-field and patriot grave, to every living heart and
hearthstone, all over this broad land, will yet swell the chorus of the
Union, when again touched, as surely they will be, by the better angels of
our nature."[1] James Madison, in *The Federalist*, No. 51, also spoke of
angels in his defense of constitutional structures: "Ambition must be
made to counteract ambition. . . . It may be a reflection on human nature
that such devices should be necessary to control the abuses of government. But what is government itself, but the greatest of all reflections on
human nature? If men were angels no government would be necessary."[2]

The tension between these two thoughts defines the purpose of
this book. The practice of democratic politics is not based on pure reason or certain morality. Interests and values clash and must be reconciled through politics rather than intellectual or moral dictates. But
reason and morality are undeniably present in politics and provide
direction for political actions. We are not angels, but we may at times
be better versions of ourselves, which was what Lincoln was calling
on Americans to be.

The central inquiry of this book is how political leaders effectively combine political arts and skills with intellectual and moral leadership. Political leadership must contain a moral element if it is to be fully effective. The talented politician must also be artful in using strategies and tactics that appeal to the interests of others as they understand them. But craft dissolves into cleverness without a clear sense of moral purpose. And significant achievements in politics and policy require a sense of shared values and goals. The same relationship between art and morals holds for the character of politicians. A good man is not necessarily a good politician. A clever politician is not necessarily a good man. But a full and complete political leader must combine elements of craft and moral purpose in his character as well as his work. Neither is sufficient in itself. This is not to deny the imperfections and flaws of character that attend political ambition. It is to affirm that moral character is itself a skill and thus a component of effective leadership.

Shakespeare depicts Julius Caesar as an artful leader, infected by hubris and thus surrendering to lesser parts of his character. Brutus is a good man, without political art, who discovers that goodness alone cannot fill the vacuum of power caused by Caesar's death. He is displaced and destroyed by the demagogue Mark Antony and the aspiring dictator Octavius Caesar. Caesar's assassination leads to the death of the republic, which is the opposite of Brutus's intention, and we are left with the puzzling question of whether the murdered man might not have been a stronger force for good than the men who seize power after his death.[3] Yet Caesar was a political man, and ambitious politicians can do us harm. We require the talent, but fear the artfulness. We wish skill to be combined with morality and yet tire of unskillful leaders, no matter how moral they are. Thus power and morals coexist uneasily, and we hope for both in our leaders.

Demagogues, who deliberately deceive us, and dictators, who would rule us, are excluded from this company, as are prophets and saints. Such leadership does not contribute to the resolution of social conflict through "politics," by which I mean the search for unity, on matters at hand, within the diversity of society.[4] Politicians must make themselves stronger than demagogues and potential dictators through their own strategies of leadership. Politicians may wish to heed and may often learn from prophets and saints, but politics is about approximations rather than absolutes and the highest ideals must be brought down to earth. Franklin Roosevelt understood the gap between reality and the ideal when he remarked that Lincoln "was a sad man because he couldn't get it all at once, and nobody can."[5]

This chapter explores a conception of political leadership, derived from the works of Aristotle and Machiavelli, that joins the necessary elements of realism and idealism. In the *Politics* and *Ethics*, Aristotle considers what is required to lead the "polity," a form of government that links oligarchy and democracy. Neither of them is desirable in itself, but combining them by artful design and leadership can result in a system of government in which the practice of politics creates unity among citizens while respecting their diversity. Machiavelli, in *The Discourses*, works within Aristotle's model of the polity and hopes for a "virtuous" union of citizens and leaders. But he reaches farther than Aristotle for the dark aspects of politics in his concern that unity be maintained. Aristotle understands that enlightened leaders must adapt their teaching to the historical community in which they work. But Machiavelli accepts demagogy and deception as perhaps necessary features of virtuous government. The Aristotelian ideal, with which I adhere, must come to terms with the Machiavellian darkness.

I make no claim that modern politics and political leadership may be understood through the works of these thinkers alone. Rather, the framework for my analysis of contemporary political leadership rests on the continuing validity of their insights.

Shakespeare created the character of a politician in King Henry V, whose style of leadership is an artful blend of morality and guile as he speaks for the nation even as he defends his patrimonial claim to lands in France. An analysis of Henry's leadership sets the stage for a discussion of modern politicians who combine personal ambition with a search for the public good.

❖ ❖ ❖

ARISTOTLE AND THE POLITY

Aristotle charges his "statesman" with the responsibility of teaching citizens about "the spirit of their constitution," or the particular system of laws under which they live.[6] The statesman does not invoke moral absolutes to cowed or deferential citizens. Rather, he must evoke those values and beliefs that citizens implicitly hold and apply them to the solution of particular problems. The culture is assumed to instill moral purpose, and the politician thus has a moral obligation to make "politics" work so that the given system of government will realize "the better angels" of its history and purpose. Aristotle regards such statesmanship as required in those forms of government whose collective purpose is the good of the whole body of citizens.

Aristotle's understanding of politics, and the roles of leaders and citizens in politics, provides an empirical and normative framework for my analysis of political leadership in American democracy. His model of the "polity" and the tasks of leadership within it touches on many of our dilemmas and possibilities. But there certainly are differences between Aristotle's conception of the good polity and the ideals of modern liberal democracy. Aristotle believed that the goal of every polis is to nurture the morally good life for all its citizens. Thus statesmen have to have high moral character along with their political skills; character is a skill because its absence is detrimental to good government. We will have to decide how much of Aristotle's ideal must be jettisoned as we develop ideas about democratic leadership. But we may also find ideas in his political philosophy that can and should be added to our democratic theory.

The Polis

Aristotle is critical of Plato's ideal state, as described in the *Republic*, because enforced uniformity prevents the diversity necessary for a real polis, which must be an aggregation of varieties of people in order to be economically and socially self-sufficient.[7] But, according to Aristotle, the polis exists for a good higher than that of the division of labor. Its primary goal should be to make it possible for citizens to live the good life of moderation, reason, and contemplation.[8] The task of good government, then, is to find moral unity in a diverse society, and here Aristotle invents the idea of politics as the means to achieve the good in society.[9] In the final analysis, politics and ethics are not separate pursuits because moral virtues can fully develop only in properly constructed political communities.[10]

The belief that virtue is learned only in community, in a polis, was shared by Greek political thinkers, but we need not adopt that view. In both the Christian and modern secular worlds, moral demands transcend those of the polity because they originate elsewhere. But, having made that qualification, we return to Aristotle's insight that transcendent morality may be realized in practice for the community only through politics.   •

Politics is thus embedded in history. Political principles are not to be sought solely through the abstract reasoning of philosophy, but through social experience. A sense of discernment of the right course of action in a particular context is crucial for good politics.[11] Since the aim of the polis is the good life for its citizens, rulers must rule for the good of the ruled. In wrongly constituted regimes, they rule only for themselves.[12]

Aristotle thus rejects tyranny, oligarchy, and democracy as bad regimes because in each the interests of one faction dominate over the good of the whole. He thinks it possible for monarchy, aristocracy, and the polity to serve the general interest.[13] He admits the possible superiority of rule by a truly good king or aristocratic elite, but decides that since humans are fallible it is best if they are governed by law rather than the discretion of rulers.[14] The rule of law is implicit in Aristotle's tenet that in order to be a good ruler a person must be able to be ruled. Mutuality, under law, is the key to good government.[15]

Singapore.

Aristotle is not a democrat in the modern sense. The citizens of his polis are those who can engage directly in the deliberations of government and serve in public offices. Freedom is thus understood to be the relations of free citizens in a polity in which men are both subject and sovereign.[16] But, even more, Aristotle regards democracy as what we would refer to as a mass society, in which respect for the variety of individuals is weak.[17] Therefore, he rests his hopes on the polity as both desirable and attainable, although still rare. But elements of the polity can be fashioned in oligarchies and democracies by tempering each system of government with the virtues of the other. In oligarchy, the wealthy rule; in democracy, the poor rule: thus each system rests on an incomplete understanding of justice. Neither wealth nor numbers is the end of political association.[18] The polity therefore should be organized on the principle of the mean and should contain both oligarchical and democratic elements, but subordinate them to the greater good. Aristotle writes: "It [polity] should owe its stability to its own intrinsic strength . . . and its intrinsic strength should be derived from the fact, not that a majority are in favor of its continuance (that might well be the case even with a poor constitution) but rather that there is no single section in the state which would favor a change to a different constitution."[19]

Aristotle cites historical evidence that a polity with a large middle class would be the strongest kind of government. Middle-class people favor a mean between the claims of wealth and those of poverty, and they suffer less from undue ambition or irrationality than those on the extremes. A polity of peers is one conducive to a community based on "friendship."[20]

The polity, though, can be a blend of social classes or of numerically different groups, or a combination of moral and intellectual qualities or of each of these blends in different political functions. J.G.A. Pocock refers to the "fruitful ambiguity" of Aristotle's vision of the polity: "The looseness of Aristotelian language was also its richness; it was capable of pursuing analysis in many directions, if it was also capable of getting those directions mixed up."[21]

The task is to reconcile the activities of people who bring separate interests to politics but whose citizenship can be sustained only if they accept the values they hold in common and treat one another in moral ways. The responsibility of political leaders, then, is to persuade the rich to respect the needs of the poor and the poor to respect the contributions of the rich. And this is to be done through politics.[22] The standard of right action in the polity is not just satisfying whatever claims are made on the state, but assessing those claims in terms of a conception of the good of all.

Leadership

Aristotle's thoughts on political leadership are scattered throughout the *Politics* and his other writings in unsystematic form, but a coherent code for governing can be discerned. He gives greater attention to the work of the statesman or lawgiver, who would fashion a good constitution at its inception, than to that of the politician. Indeed, he describes politicians as demagogues who speak for only segments of the whole, and thus unjustly. But his advice to statesmen is also clearly intended for governing elites who must sustain a polity by practice.

The trait that Aristotle values in leaders above all is "prudence."[23] This is the one characteristic that citizens need not have but that rulers must have. Prudence is practical wisdom about how to balance and accommodate competing interests in a constitution. The art and craft of statesmanship are just like the work of physicians, who seek the health of their patients. By the same token, statesmen seek the good of the polis. If a politician tries to help his friends or punish his enemies, he forfeits his claim to govern.[24]

Aristotle sees a reciprocal relationship between prudent leaders and the body of citizens because whereas individual citizens lack prudence, when they come together to deliberate they may surpass, collectively, the quality of the few best men. Citizens may be reliable judges of the merits of what government does, even if they may lack the prudence to join means and ends to produce such results.[25]

Statesmen must keep in mind not only the absolute best, but the best in the historical context.[26] The practical wisdom needed by statesmen is not formal knowledge based on "demonstrative reasoning" without thought of contingencies because "all matters of deliberation must be contingent."[27] Practical wisdom is anchored in the details of life: "And so one should attend to the undemonstrable dicta and opinion of the skillful, the old and practically wise, no less than those which are based on strict reasoning, because they see aright, having gained their power of moral vision from experience."[28] Thus practical wisdom is not the same as cleverness and cannot attain its objectives without "goodness" because "vice distorts the moral vision and causes men to be deceived in respect of practical principles. . . . A man cannot be practically wise without being a good man."[29] Aristotle adds that those who live "in obedience to passion will not listen to advice that might dissuade them from acting wrongly."[30]

Wise leaders should seek the "mean" in practice. Democrats and oligarchs push to extremes; intelligent leaders must temper such claims to counter both demagogues, who urge war against the rich, and oligarchs, who ignore the needs of the poor.[31] The solutions to such conflicts are not, however, to be found in philosophy, for "to find theoretically where truth resides in these matters of equality and justice is a very difficult task."[32] Prudence may be adept at finding practical solutions to problems for which there are no theoretical answers.

It is both the virtue and the ambiguity of this formulation of the importance of the common good and the difficulty of achieving it that give staying power to Aristotle's conception of politics. There is a common good to be discovered, but it is not often, if ever, known at the outset. Rather, it must be achieved through approximations and nourished by politics. But that does not make the common good any less desirable or important as a goal. Political theories of modern democracy have not improved on Aristotle's analysis.

Aristotle thus recognizes the practical importance of a leader's discernment of historical context as he works to accomplish social goals.[33] Dialectical inquiry begins with the diversity of opinions, and insights emerge from continual conversations about a given history, culture, and language grounded in the experience of many people over a considerable time.[34] Aristotle speaks for those who would combine principles with practice without sacrificing either. The good for people, the virtues of the mean, can be realized in a variety of forms; therefore, following Aristotle, we might well think of the polity as a protean reality with many possible expressions.[35] For example, a debate between adherents of liberal individualism and republican communitarianism in contemporary politics perhaps cannot be resolved in theory, but may be settled in practice as both sides admit the practical deficiencies of their own abstractions and agree in concrete terms, if not in theory. For example, the path from welfare to work would provide incentives to work but security from want.

By the same token, our political language is enriched if we follow Aristotle in acknowledging that "interests" and "virtues" are inextricably linked in real life. If we regard politics as simply a clash of interests, then we can understand it only as a series of endless "prisoner's dilemma" games in which the search for personal or group utility prevails. For Aristotle, interest and virtue are not mutually exclusive. Rather, interests are assessed according to how they serve human needs, seen ultimately in terms of the good.[36]

Aristotle's view of politics may be characterized as a continuing debate about the nature of justice. The definition of justice is elusive, but develops among people who have an equal share in ruling and being ruled. Communities are unified by reciprocity.[37] In this sense, political leaders are both creatures of their environment, who must work within tolerable limits set by the equilibrium of interests and values, and creators of a new understanding of the "spirit of the constitution" and thus of new social equilibria. Aristotle's recognition of the importance, but elusiveness, of the good and of the necessary combination of practical reason and moral aspiration, and his belief that political analysis must work within given historical contexts, recommend him as a guide to contemporary political leaders.

❖ ❖ ❖

MACHIAVELLI AND THE PRINCIPALITY AND REPUBLIC

Niccolò Machiavelli addresses two kinds of states and their politics: the principality and the republic. His central questions are how a prince may win control of a state and the obedience of its citizens, and how a republic may be stable and enduring. He gives more attention to leadership than does Aristotle because he regards it as the key to political health and stability. However, the paths to stability are very different in principalities and republics.

Machiavelli's ideas were part of the revival of the Greek republican ideal by "civic humanists" of the Renaissance.[38] He wrote within an Aristotelian framework, but with even greater concern than Aristotle for understanding the ingredients of political stability, as his civic world was continually in turmoil. *The Prince* is a collection of insights and propositions for princes who would establish and maintain their rule in all sorts of states. It begins with the assumption that seemingly immoral actions may be required of a ruler who is good, since he will surely be at a disadvantage in a world in which most men are not good.[39] The canons of private morality are of little use to those who would rule. Machiavelli does not praise villainy and immorality for their own sakes, however; both are means to a good end. A resourceful leader must use stratagems to win and keep power. A kind of amorality is advised in which the prince remains detached from the instruments of rule. Murder and violence, duplicity and manipulation are to be invoked only when they have utility. Such actions are on the same moral plane as mercy, magnanimity, and beneficence. Indeed, the authority of a prince is the strongest when he has the support of his people.[40]

Political skill thus is essential to political success, and yet Machiavelli understands that *fortuna*, the contingent in history, provides not only opportunities for the skillful, but also constraints on historical freedom to act. Skill is more or less effective as the context changes.[41]

The Prince is a primer that Machiavelli wrote separately from *The Discourses,* but considered as only one part of a larger whole, in which his greatest concern is how to revive the classical republican tradition in Renaissance Italy. Machiavelli takes the Roman republic as his model. He adds the element of virtuous citizens, which is only a mild refrain in *The Prince*. The combination of good institutions and citizens with great civic virtue may render the bloody rule of the prince unnecessary. Machiavelli respects a mixed constitution in which segments of the citizenry are represented in different institutions and the whole is maintained by a dynamic tension among the constituent groups. As opposing forces support an arch, the health of a republic is rooted in the support it receives from all factions in preference to any other form of government.[42]

Aristotle in no way glorifies the leaders of the good polity. But Machiavelli must do so because he wishes the glory and power of the state to be an end in itself in a way that Aristotle condemns. Machiavelli envisions his republic as an "armed, popular state" that can mobilize its citizens for civic and military purposes.[43] The republic is to pursue empire, and therefore its best resource is the citizen soldier, rather than a professional military. Only in republics can citizens be mobilized for such a public good. In this sense, the message of *The Discourses* may be even more amoral than that of *The Prince*.[44]

The principal task of political leadership in a republic is to articulate the glory of the state to its citizens. Machiavelli reaches beyond the Aristotelian framework and advocates political demagoguery as a means to political unity and action. Political leaders must articulate "myths" about the state if it is to be unified and dynamic. Machiavelli would discard the Christian ethic in favor of a civil religion that, as in Roman times, would be an inspiration to citizen soldiers.[45]

The skillful political leader must govern, in part, by appearances. If he displays grandeur, spirit, gravity, and fortitude, it will be difficult for dissidents to unseat him, for he will have a hold on the popular affections. A strong figure who can appeal to patriotism will be invincible. A devotion to glory, as opposed to simply seeking to dominate, will provide a sold base for accountability between people and their leaders. Those who win power will act to sustain the myths by which they ascended as long as the people they govern believe in the myths.[46]

He also believes, with Aristotle, that a free people, who possess civic virtue, will defend their liberty against those who would violate it.[47] Civic virtue develops historically and turns people, who may be individually weak, into strong citizens when they act in concert. But even so, a free people requires leaders who will match their skills against the contingencies of *fortuna*.[48] There is no substitute for prudence in a politician who must have great discernment in matching means to ends.[49] Like Aristotle, Machiavelli does not believe that the correctness of prudent action can be deduced from an authoritative body of knowledge. The skill of prudence must come from astuteness and experience.[50]

Hannah Pitkin sees Machiavelli's search for new bases of authority as a departure from the ascriptive hierarchy and mutual dependence of the higher and lower orders of the medieval world. He articulates the Renaissance ideal of "human self-creation," in which the individual shapes himself and others through historical action. She concludes that Machiavelli's understanding of politics is similar to Aristotle's teaching that man is a political animal who must engage in politics to be fully human. People are capable of free action within the bounds of necessity. The task of leadership is to keep the state on an even keel. In particular, the leader with great political virtuosity rises above Aristotle's polity and becomes, for Machiavelli, the absolute key to the strength of the state. He must demonstrate flexibility and adaptation to changing historical circumstances as he faces contingencies and *fortuna* in an uncertain world.[51]

Machiavelli clearly breaks with Aristotle's belief that while all societies are imperfect some societies may be able to nurture a good life of reason and moderation for citizens. The state is its own end for Machiavelli.[52] Harvey Mansfield suggests in this context that Machiavelli invents the modern "worldly executive," who will "execute the decree of natural necessity" as the realpolitik of the state is served.[53] Such virtuosity must be free of law because it responds to necessity, and justice is only one resource among several, some of which are antithetical to it.[54] Machiavelli thus presents us with one of the first statements of the modern problem of the political accountability of executive leaders in a chaotic world. Aristotle places leadership within the mantle of law, and Machiavelli raises virtuosity above the law.[55]

Aristotle and Machiavelli complement each other nicely for my purposes. Aristotle presents us with the task of political leadership in a polity, which is to combine practical reason, custom, and morality in ways that unite, rather than divide, citizens. There is a moral good, by which the polity should steer, but there is no authoritative interpretation of that good; politics is a continuing conversation throughout the polity about how to achieve what is thought to be good within a concrete polity and history. Machiavelli begins with that framework and expresses confidence in mixed institutions and the unity from diversity that they may foster. But he divorces the enterprise from any search for the good, other than the strength of the state, and gives his rulers a license for demagoguery that is not found in Aristotle.

We cannot just accept Aristotle and dismiss Machiavelli because the modern polity contains all the possibilities that both theorists describe. If we are to follow Aristotle, we must understand how to avoid the pitfalls of the Machiavellian polity, in theory and in practice. We must ask if it is possible for modern political leaders, in our democratic polities, to avoid Machiavelli's methods as they seek to achieve Aristotle's goals. These two thinkers give us a rich framework for inquiry and analysis about democratic leadership today.

❖ ❖ ❖

SHAKESPEARE'S POLITICIANS

William Shakespeare created many political characters who stand alone as classic types of leaders: Richard III is an archvillain; Coriolanus, a soldier who will not stoop to seek political favor from the crowd; Henry VI, an otherworldly ruler who forfeits his burdens; and Macbeth, a heroic usurper. But he also created characters in clusters, so we cannot fully understand the actions of one character without understanding how the members of a group of people influence one another. And, reaching beyond little knots of characters, he gives us historical dramas that follow the unfolding of a theme that also controls his actors. The guiding theme of his historical plays about the English kings during the Wars of the Roses is the search for the legitimacy of royal authority, which finally culminates in the Tudor monarchs and English unity.

The playwright portrays Machiavellian heros and villains who exist, in his conception, not only to illustrate moral themes in English history but also as embodiments of perennial truths about leadership. In this sense, Shakespeare is something of a synthesis of Aristotle and

Machiavelli. He asks politicians to be both good and clever. Neither weakness nor immorality is legitimate. Even more important, the ideal polity is one of legitimacy and order. The idea that anarchy is the norm in politics was foreign to Shakespeare.[56]

We feel a shock of recognition when confronted by Shakespeare's politicians. The poet is not encumbered by the historians' standard of factual accuracy and can create and interpret historical characters who embody the different ways in which political men choose to do their work.[57] Practicing politicians would do well to study the flaws of character and errors of practice of Shakespeare's politicians, as well as their virtues.[58]

We learn in the historical plays that statecraft and moral virtue are complementary and that neither will suffice alone to guarantee effectiveness. To the extent that this insight is true, Shakespeare speaks to us today. Henry V is a complete politician who "is from the very first a commanding character, deliberate in act and judgement, versed in every phase of human nature."[59] In one sense, then, Henry is the idealization of a Renaissance prince, Shakespeare playing up to the Tudor and Stuart kings of his time; but in another sense, he is a political man who must be taken as he is. Shakespeare knew what sort of man would be most effective in political life, and, in his portrait of Henry, he gives us such a man.[60]

We must place Henry in the historical context of civil war. His father, Bolingbroke, had seized the crown from Richard II, a weak and spiteful king, and for that reason lacked legitimacy. In *Richard II*, Richard is depicted as the last king of the passing medieval order, which is being succeeded by a time of turbulence, disorder, and misrule.[61] It is a world of conflict among dangerous, self-centered men, in which the stakes are life and death.

Bolingbroke is portrayed as a "politician" as the Elizabethans understood the term, a self-seeker who is ruled by his ambition.[62] Richard, although weak, is also imperious and thus undermines his authority by imprudent actions. The king has banished Bolingbroke from England in the aftermath of a dispute with another knight. But when Boling-

broke's father, John of Gaunt, dies, Richard seizes his property, Bolingbroke's rightful inheritance, to support his wars in Ireland. Before he
dies, John of Gaunt captures Richard's self-centeredness:

> A thousand flatterers sit within thy crown,
> Whose compass is no bigger than thy head.[63]

Richard is warned that he should not violate the laws of inheritance, but pays no heed and goes to Ireland. Bolingbroke then returns
to England with an army, and, through mishaps, Richard loses his
army and is captured. Bolingbroke asks the king for the return of his
property, and Richard agrees. But Richard's will is completely broken,
and he subsequently offers his crown to his foe. Shakespeare gives us
the impression that Bolingbroke had not considered that possibility,
but he is an opportunist and responds according to his character: "In
God's name, I'll ascend the regal throne."[64] The bishop of Carlisle
warns Bolingbroke not to do so because, if he does,

> The blood of English shall manure the ground,
> And future ages groan for this foul act.[65]

The usurper responds by forcing Richard to renounce the crown publicly so that the new king may, as he says, "proceed without suspicion."[66]

Richard is murdered not long after by men hoping to please the
new king, who vows to make a pilgrimage to the Holy Land "to wash
this blood off from my guilty hand."[67] He has triumphed, but is
unsure of the foundations of his power.[68] However, Henry IV has
strong political skills, which are seen when he rebukes a court of
unruly peers who fall out like a pack of dogs among themselves. He
knows that he can trust none of them. We have entered the world of
Machiavelli's prince.[69]

In *Henry IV*, Parts 1 and 2, Shakespeare presents the king as a
strong man who lacks guiding principles beyond the preservation of
his throne. He is a political opportunist.[70] As he is dying, he tells his
son, Hal, of the uncertainty of his authority because of how it was
obtained:

> God knows, my son,
> By what bypaths and indirect crooked ways
> I met this crown, and I myself know well
> How troublesome it sat upon my head.
> To thee it shall descend with better quiet,
> Better opinion, better confirmation,
> For all the soil of the achievement goes
> With me into the earth.[71]

Henry IV is pathetic and bewildered and without moorings precisely because he has relied too much on his own strength and fortune. His reign has been one of political disorder because he has not been able to govern according to shared purposes.[72]

Henry V has his own play, but he is also the central character of the two parts of *Henry IV*. The three plays together present a picture of the development of a political man to maturity. We first meet Hal as a prodigal son who spends his time in taverns with Sir John Falstaff and other reprobates. Although he enjoys the low life, Hal keeps a certain detachment from it, even as he learns about the lives of ordinary people. He tells his fellows:

> I know you all, and will a while uphold
> The unyoked humor of your idleness.
> Yet herein will I imitate the sun,
> Who doth permit the base contagiouss clouds,
> To smother up his beauty from the world,
> That, when he please again to be himself,
> Being wanted, he may be more wond'red at
>
> . . .
>
> By so much shall I falsify men's hopes;
> And, like bright metal on a sullen ground,
> My reformation, glitt'ring o'er my fault
> Shall show more goodly and attract more eyes
> Than that which hath no foil to set it off.
> I'll so offend to make offense a skill,
> Redeeming time when men think least I will.[73]

Falstaff and his company are Hal's link between the two worlds of everyday humanity and the narrow life of the court. Hal is preparing for the throne even as he enjoys himself.[74] As the king laments his son's escapades, Warwick tells him that all will be well:

> The prince but studies his companions
> Like a strange tongue, wherein, to gain the language,
>
> . . .
>
> The prince will in the perfectness of time
> Cast off his followers, and their memory
> Shall as a pattern or a measure live,
> By which his grace must mete the lives of others,
> Turning past evils to advantages.[75]

Hal is called from the tavern to help his father overcome a rebellion of lords in the north and, during that fight, confronts one of the rebels, Henry Percy (Hotspur), the son of the duke of Northumberland. Hotspur fights for honor and is completely lacking in prudence. When they meet on the field, Hal tells Hotspur that there is not enough room in England for both of them, and kills him.[76]

Falstaff and Hotspur present the extremes to which Hal is to be the mean. He exhibits "a creative will that points toward a new kind of world."[77] It has been suggested that the prince, and his creator, are following "the theme of Aristotle's *Ethics:* virtue as the mean between two extremes of conduct."[78] Falstaff is mired in ordinary life, and Hotspur is lost in the outdated world of chivalry, whereas Hal is unfolding a personality "that develops in Aristotelian fashion from potentiality to essence."[79]

By the time he becomes king, Henry V has lived in both Falstaff's and Hotspur's worlds and has assumed the legacy of his father without limiting himself in any way. He becomes a king around whom the English, Scots, Welsh, and Irish can rally.[80] Of course, this may not be difficult when their common objective is to kill Frenchmen.

Hal is reconciled with his father as the old king dies. But he must repudiate Falstaff, who assumes that he will be elevated. Rather, the corrupt old knight is met with fierce brutality from his former friend:

> I know you not, old man. . . .
> Presume not that I am the thing I was.[81]

Henry also tells the chief justice of England, whom he once assaulted, that he is a new man:

> The tide of blood in me
> Hath proudly flowed in vanity till now.
> Now it doth turn and ebb back to the sea,
> Where it shall mingle with the state of floods
> And flow henceforth in formal majesty.
> Now call we our high court of parliament,
> And let us choose such limbs of noble counsel
> That the great body of our state may go
> In equal rank with the best-governed nation.[82]

And as *Henry IV* ends, there is a hint that before long Henry V will lead an army to France to recover lost royal lands. The depiction of Henry V in his own play could be read as Shakespeare's idealization of the perfect king. One critic contends that the writer had to abandon the flesh-and-blood Hal in order to meet the expectations of his audiences for an Elizabethan hero.[83] However, beneath the ideal exterior is a highly realistic portrait of a talented and opportunistic political man.

By the time *Henry V* opens, the king has manipulated the archbishop of Canterbury into advocating Henry's right to invade France in order to recoup the royal lands. Of course, the divine has his own motives, one of which is to avoid taxation of the church, and the king knows that. Henry wants to invade France, but only with due authority.[84] He then contrives a situation in which he can disclaim personal responsibility for sending three nobles, who have plotted against him, to their deaths. He tricks them into advising no mercy for traitors and thus catches them in the trap they have helped prepare. Henry is good at putting his enemies in the wrong.[85] We are then presented with a heroic leader in France who is propelled by a dynastic motive but disguises private purpose with the rhetoric of nationalism and heroism.

For him, war is an instrument of policy, but his soldiers are fighting for their country.[86] Henry is the subtle politician as actor who knows the right word and gesture for every occasion. His observing detachment has taught him how to manipulate audiences.[87]

He is conscious of his father's crime, and the night before the battle prays that God may erase it if he reburies Richard's body in a suitable place.[88] But in the morning, as he speaks to his army, Henry is the eloquent English king:

> We few, we happy few, we band of brothers;
> For he that sheds his blood with me
> Shall be my brother, be he ne'er so vile,
> This day shall gentle his condition.
> And gentlemen in England, now abed,
>   Shall think themselves accursed they were not here;
> And hold their manhood cheap whiles any speaks
> That fought with us upon Saint Crispin's day.[89]

Henry tells those who do not wish to fight that they may freely return home, or they may seek honors with him, for

> . . . if it be a sin to covet honor,
> I am the most offending soul alive.[90]

E.M.W. Tillyard quotes George Orwell on heroic characters to illustrate Henry's leadership: "The high sentiments always win in the end; leaders who offer blood, toil, tears and sweat always get more out of their followers than those who offer safety and a good time. When it comes to the pinch human beings are heroic."[91]

Shakespeare is telling us what a political hero must do. But he also shows us, with sympathy, the frailty of the man who feels his father's guilt and admits to some of his soldiers, while walking through the camp at night in disguise, "I think the king is but a man, as I am: . . . His ceremonies laid by, in his nakedness he appears but a man. . . . Yet, in reason, no man should possess him with any appearance of fear, lest he, by showing it, should dishearten his army."[92]

Henry has learned to present his royal persona in order to lead. He

draws love to himself but gives little back, and his detachment permits him to discipline his actions to his purpose.[93] Shakespeare gives
us a picture of a talented political man whom we may understand at
different levels. He is an idealized heroic king. He is an accomplished
actor. He is detached from all men, but can stir men's hearts. And,
finally, he can transform his private motives into public causes.[94]
Shakespeare does not judge him as much as draw a picture of great
political virtuosity. He is as he is.

The triumph of Henry V gives way to the failure of his son, Henry
VI, with the clear lesson that the Wars of the Roses will continue until
the stain of Bolingbroke is wiped away. It is not until Richard III is
dethroned by the earl of Richmond, of the House of Lancaster, who
marries into the House of York, that the country is reunited. Henry of
Richmond, along with Malcolm in *Macbeth* and Edgar in *King Lear*,
ascends legitimately to power as the Tudor king Henry VII.[95] Tillyard
suggests that Henry V cannot be Shakespeare's "ideal reigning king"
because of his father's crime. However in Malcolm, the rightful heir
of the slain Duncan, he finds a good king, and thus *Macbeth* is "the
epilogue of the histories." The body politic as a whole has defeated
Macbeth. A villain has been exposed and punished, and a legitimate
king now rules. In *The Tempest*, perhaps his last play, Shakespeare
affirms his hope that justice and mercy will be combined in rulers.
Prospero finds an Aristotelian mean between reason and passion, for-
giveness and revenge.[96]

Shakespeare does not preach but tells us about life in all its richness. Uncertainties about the relationship between power and virtue
are inherent in his understanding of political life. Somehow, the two
must be combined for effective rule, but it is not easily done.

Shakespeare's kings live in Machiavelli's world. His portraits are
not unlike those that Machiavelli draws, although they are far richer
and more complex. They are also of essential types of political leaders
who can be found in the modern world. Aristotle does not depict such
leaders, nor would he have approved of them. But today's world must
have political leaders who stand alone to some extent, for better or
worse. And, therefore, Shakespeare's politicians are relevant to us. To

what extent can they be reconciled with the demands of prudence and wisdom in Aristotle's polity?

THE MODERN POLITICIAN

This book argues that truth telling, empowerment, and altruism in politics are not only desirable, but practical and achievable in history. Demagogy and deception are present in much political persuasion, even in the best polities, but truth is enabling because it better conforms to reality than falsehood. F. G. Bailey disagrees, arguing that political appeals transcend both truth and falsehood: "The essence of leadership is a capacity to go beyond rationality to operate by intuition, and to obliterate scientific search for objective fact . . . and at the same time to convince the followers that [the leader] knows what he is doing."[97]

Political rhetoric is thus said to claim more than it knows and to use evidence to buttress appeals to magic and myth. Bailey regards leadership as "the art of exploiting cultures" to carry an argument successfully. To *exploit* culture is to use the best arguments at hand, whether true or not. To *teach* culture is to ask citizens to be "the better angels of [their] nature." This book affirms the realism of teaching, but on what grounds? Why should the virtuous win? I cannot prove my point; it is an act of faith. And faith resides in a sense of confidence about culture. It is a faith that the strongest ideals in national political culture will be continually invoked as a basis for action and that the citizens of that culture will rise to the occasion if they believe in those ideals. However, I confine this view to my understanding of the American polity.

There is a dynamic in American society that forces the recognition and resolution of the perennial American tension between liberty and equality. According to the exigencies of the time, our politics and public policies move back and forth in the emphasis given to one or the other. Gunnar Myrdal wrote in *An American Dilemma* that Americans would solve the problem of racial injustice or they would cease to be Americans.[98] But American political culture also contains blind spots that seemingly are never erased. Our exaggerated individualism does not protect the weak or curb the strong who hide behind it. There is thus fundamental injustice in American society at all times, and it could be the consequence of our adherence to our very cultural ideals. Perhaps political leaders who would teach "the spirit of the constitution" must skip over the blind spots if they are to be effective. Or perhaps palliatives for the lapses are invented from generation to generation. This understanding of cultural leadership makes sense only if we assume that politics is animated by understanding, perhaps in partial and limited ways, of a national purpose or purposes toward which we grope. There is nothing inevitable about this process of rediscovery and affirmation. It happens only through the spontaneous and uncoordinated actions of many citizens and leaders, including politicians, over a long period of time.

Max Weber depicted the ideal, and yet very real, democratic politician in his essay "Politics as a Vocation." Weber regarded politics, at its best, as something more than the advocacy of interests. To him, a political career offered, above all, an opportunity to participate in historically important events. That was a far stronger motive for entering politics than the service of interests or the pursuit of power. Weber considered the kind of person who should be permitted to "put his hand on the wheel of history" and set three requirements: "passion, a feeling of responsibility, and a sense of proportion."[99] He must be passionate if the work is not to be frivolous, but also must have an "inner concentration and calmness"—hence a certain need for detachment—that permits him to see events in perspective. Above all, he must avoid "self-intoxication," which is the classic vice of the politician. If a politician cares only about "the impression that he makes," his work "leads nowhere and is senseless." An inner weakness hides behind the "boastful but empty gesture." The good politician must be both engaged and detached, and must see his work in the context of the given historical moment; the truly forceful and effective politician must also carry moral commitment.[100]

The political leader who can appeal to national ideals will win more often than the demagogue. Under certain historical conditions, which will be explored later, idealism is the strongest possible political appeal that leaders can invoke. But must not such leaders do exactly what Bailey says all leaders must do: appeal to intuition beyond rationality? Is this not deception? I think not. Political rhetoric must necessarily claim more than it knows and call for collective action without blueprints of implementation. But when the appeal is to the deepest ideals of the society, its authenticity will be honored. Considerations of compromise to achieve political agreement and subordination of ambition to practicality must be respected. We stay within what we know how to do when we act to implement our ideals. But the authenticity of the ideals themselves is not diminished by considerations of practicality.

Consider the leadership of Abraham Lincoln. He was a supremely skilled politician who could have not been elected president in 1860 had he campaigned for the abolition of slavery. And yet his moral disapproval of slavery was profound. His solution was to support the Union and limit the expansion of slavery. His political sagacity was revealed in his shrewd letter to Horace Greeley, the New York editor who called on Lincoln to abolish slavery. Lincoln replied that his objective was to save the Union. If he could do so by abolishing slavery, he would. If it could best be done without abolishing slavery, he would follow that path. Greeley was trying to force Lincoln's hand to issue the Emancipation Proclamation, which Greeley knew was in Lincoln's desk drawer. But Lincoln would not be pushed. As Garry Wills says, "this is the highest art which conceals itself."[101] Lincoln was waiting for the moment at which issuing the proclamation could best be justified by the practical task of winning the war. And the historian Richard Hofstadter thus wrote that the Emancipation Proclamation had "all the moral grandeur of a bill of lading."[102] William Safire, in his novel *Freedom*, has John Hay ask of Lincoln at the time of the exchange with Greeley: "he hates to be seen leading. He wants to 'shoo' others in front. But can a 'shooer' be a leader?"[103]

Yet Wills insists that Lincoln's Gettysburg Address reinterpreted the American historical experience according to the Declaration of

Independence and thus set the Constitution within a new moral and political frame. The purpose of the Union was now more than to provide a constitutional government for all citizens. It was also to make freedom accessible to all Americans. Wills argues that Lincoln created a "new political prose for America," much as Mark Twain created a new American literature by writing in the vernacular. He did it "by sleight of hand" in 272 words. But those words stood behind the Fourteenth Amendment, which has transformed our law and politics, despite all the failures to fully realize its ideals.

David Greenstone broadens the portrait of Lincoln by depicting him as the one politician who achieved a reinterpretation of American values that eluded other leaders of his generation. He leavened American individualism with a humanitarianism that had always been present but latent, a sense of the community as the guarantor of liberty for all. All forms of separatism were to be rejected, and all individuals were to be redeemed. Black Americans had to be included in the dream.[104]

The historian Benjamin Thomas has described Lincoln as "cautious and conservative" and a "consummate politician." He held a wartime coalition of extreme opposites together by sheer personal skill. His own slow advancement in politics had taught him patience, and he always waited until events made leadership acceptable and then argued that the events had driven him more than he had driven them. He believed, Thomas says, that the people were wise, if they could be informed. But his leadership was so deft that many contemporaries failed to recognize it. Greeley wrote of Lincoln after his death that he had been "a great persuader" who "was open to all impressions and influences. . . . There was probably no year of his life when he was not a wiser, cooler, and better man than he had been in the year proceeding."[105] Lincoln taught us "the spirit of the constitution."

Lincoln is a dramatic and seemingly atypical politician to use to illustrate my point about the persistence and achievement of cultural ideals. But perhaps such leadership occurs in many small ways throughout the American polity, in the acts of citizens as well as political leaders. Perhaps the search for collective purposes is the business of all Americans.

2

Conceptions of Leadership

❖ ❖ ❖ ❖ ❖ ❖ ❖ ❖ ❖ ❖ ❖ ❖ ❖ ❖

Two conceptions of political action are important in American politics. The first celebrates coalition building in a pluralist polity and is disposed to a politics of balance and stability. The second evokes electoral mandates in which popular majorities, working through centralizing institutions like the presidency, are depicted as the agents of policy innovation. There is a tension between a sense of limits and a desire for boldness, but both are essential for a full expression of the possibilities of politics.

❖ ❖ ❖

STRATEGY AND SKILL IN CONTEXT

The skills required of the politician who would build bargaining coalitions are a keen sense of how others perceive their interests and the ability to fashion a coalition of such interests usually one issue at a time. The skills required of the politician who would appeal to popular majorities are to discern and evoke unresolved problems and suggest plausible remedies that reinterpret shared beliefs and values in new, appropriate ways. All politics is obviously a combination of these strategies, but the distinction is useful because the resources on which politicians rely differ, depending on their approach.

The American presidency has been analyzed and explained in terms of both conceptions, in which the president is sometimes a lion and other times a fox. The lion emerges from "progressive" ideas about presidential leadership in modern American history, in which the president, as popular tribune for reform, is ascendant. Woodrow Wilson's words, written before he became president, capture the spirit:

His is the only national force in affairs. Let him once win the admiration and confidence of the country, and no other single force can withstand him.

. . . [T]he country never feels the zest for action so much as when its President is of such insight and calibre. Its instinct is for unified action and it craves a single leader.

The President is at liberty, both in law and conscience, to be as big a man as he can. His capacity will set the limit; and if Congress be overborne by him, it will be no fault of the makers of the Constitution. . . . It will be from no lack of consitutional powers on its part, but only because the President has the nation behind him, and Congress has not. He has no means of compelling Congress except through public opinion.[1]

In 1937, Wilfred Binkley, writing in the same vein, cited Franklin Roosevelt's words that the presidency is not primarily an administrative office, but "preeminently a place of moral leadership. All our great presidents were leaders of thought at times when certain historic ideas in the life of the nation had to be clarified."[2] But Binkley wrote just as Congress was beginning to take the measure of Roosevelt after the failure of his attempt to pack the Supreme Court. Binkley tempered the claim to heroism by an acknowledgment that presidential leadership of the kind he favored was likely to occur only in times of crisis, such as the Great Depression.

Pendleton Herring, writing just three years later, acknowledged progressive aspirations but pointed out that presidents have to be more than popular tribunes. They must find ways to bargain and persuade in close quarters. The effective president must be a "politician as well as a statesman."[3] Bargaining is the task of presidential leadership in normal times. Vision and rhetoric may fall on barren ground. The skills of the fox are then required.

This was the intellectual and historical background against which Richard Neustadt wrote *Presidential Power,* the most important book on the presidency published in the second half of the century.[4] Neustadt created the categories with which all modern presidents have been studied and evaluated. He explicitly cited Wilson, Binkley, and Herring as his antecedents.[5] But the presidency they described, so full of heroic potential, had not been the presidency he saw while working in the Truman White House. Neustadt gradually began to develop a thesis that the foundation for effective presidential leadership is not found in making heroic gestures or in brandishing constitutional powers, but in using informal strategies of persuasion in conjunction with constitutional tasks. He made his project a primer of practical advice for presidents about how they might help their influence in future situations by their actions in the present. The primary task of the president is to persuade others, who have independent power, that what they wish to achieve is compatible with his own purposes. Such influence was described metaphorically as akin to "bargaining."

The historical context for Neustadt's president was "politics at mid-century," the time of policy stalemate between the presidency and a Congress dominated by the "conservative coalition" of southern Democrats and midwestern Republicans, who had put a stop to the New Deal in 1937. The same congressional coalition opposed the enactment of the Fair Deal, despite Harry Truman's dramatic victory in 1948, and continued through the administrations of Dwight Eisenhower and John Kennedy until Lyndon Johnson broke the logjam in 1964 and 1965. As his first task, Neustadt's ideal president has to understand that decision making in the presidency is a seamless web in which each decision influences and is influenced by others. Thus Neustadt reached beyond the conception of the presidency as a collection of separate "hats," or roles, such as chief legislator and commander in chief, to the idea that all actions influence the possibility of future actions. The fact of president and Congress as "separated institutions sharing powers" is the fact of life to be confronted. Bargains have to be extracted through presidential appeals to the political incentives and policy goals of other power holders—in Congress, the cabinet, and the bureaucracies. Even presidential leadership of the public is a form of bargaining as presidents use events to teach citizens when their interests are at stake on given matters.

Neustadt asked the timeless question: How is a politician to persuade others to follow him when he knows that their purposes are, to some considerable extent, different from his? In reply, he recommended presidential self-help by which a president would make current decisions in the light of their effect on subsequent actions that he must take. President watchers would then know what to expect next time. If a president vetoed a bill, there was a good chance that he would veto another bill in a similar situation. If a White House compromise gave away too much, others would remember that and press their future claims accordingly. The president's most valuable resource is his "professional reputation" in Washington and the country.

Neustadt understood that the presidency at mid-century was not a place for heroes. However, he made Franklin Roosevelt the exemplar for all future presidents. This was ironic because FDR's great years of achievement were in his first term, when he had the political support in the country that permitted him to be both lion and fox. The first and second New Deal legislative programs were achieved against the backdrop of the severe Depression. Roosevelt's success resulted from his courageous and inspiring public leadership and his ability to work with legislative leaders and executive advisers and agents, bargaining and compromising to accomplish recovery and reform. The Roosevelt that Neustadt actually described in *Presidential Power* was the skillful and canny fox rather than the courageous lion. He was FDR the supreme manipulator, who understood that his hopes must satisfy the claims of others. The irony is that Roosevelt the fox was a much less effective president in his second term than in his first because there were severe limits to what bargaining could accomplish without the backdrop of popular support, joined to crisis, that had produced the leadership of the lion.

Neustadt's primer of advice made great sense for politics at mid-century precisely because there were not going to be any great policy innovations in such a period. Progress must necessarily be ad hoc, incremental, and, most important, a product of the skillful discernment by the president of the incentives of others. Unless a president is sensitive to not only his own power stakes in given issues, but the power stakes of other independent actors he will surely come to grief. Even so, success is not guaranteed.

Neustadt was careful not to reduce politics to questions of tangible material interests. The conception of leadership as bargaining in a pluralist world may be understood in this way because so many interest groups lobby for material claims. But Neustadt did not ignore ideology or values. All politics, whether material or spiritual, is encompassed within the world of bargains.

Early critics of Neustadt took him to task for advising his presidents to rely on instrumental appeals. They asked if it was not possible that presidents might appeal to shared beliefs. Neustadt had an answer. Even in a band of brothers, individual stakes differ, and therefore the president must recognize and appeal to such interests in all his work. Critics also argued that a bargaining president, who must discern the stakes of other important actors, would eventually collapse from overwork at rational calculation of what those stakes are. Kennedy complained that Neustadt's president would have to spend too much time in calculation. Neustadt was said to have compounded the problem by insisting that the president's assistants do not see his tasks as he sees them. They consider only their part in the overall political process. Neustadt was critical of Eisenhower for having delegated too many of his choices to others. Neustadt would argue that a president must be an expert in the politics of the issues he chooses to address—not only the interpersonal politics of Washington, but the national politics of issues. He will get much political advice, but ultimately, only the president can formulate a grand political strategy for his presidency, within which the politics of specific measures will fall.

This task cannot be delegated. Because Neustadt wrote at a time of stalemate in popular politics and thus focused primarily on the Washington world of instrumental politics, his critics failed to see that a larger, popular politics may be included in his framework as well. His ideal president is like the grand chess master who can beat several opponents in separate games at the same time because he has a repertoire of games, moves, and plays that the less experienced chess player does not possess.

James MacGregor Burns, writing in the 1970s, saw Neustadt's prescriptions for presidents as embracing only half the possibilities for leadership. Neustadt's presidents "have a choice only of options relevant to the context in which they bargain."[6] Bargaining presidents are "transactional" leaders who exchange favors during times of political stability in which fundamental questions about policy or the polity are not posed. "Transforming" leaders articulate and reinterpret the historical situations in times of uncertainty and, as they do so, appeal to revised versions of fundamental moral and political beliefs and values. This is the only way to effectively close the gap between presidential weakness and presidential aspiration. Instead, the president as transactional leader will only "dicker and transact," resulting in "endless presidential bargaining, persuading, power hoarding, managing manipulation—is this executive leadership?" For Burns, it is technique divorced from goals and values. A politics of "satisficing" is ultimately sterile:

> The resort to incrementalist, transaction types of decision-making leadership underlies . . . the plight of party, legislative, executive, and other decision makers facing crises they cannot fully comprehend, under circumstances of others' making, at times they cannot control, and without the opportunity or even the ability to exploit information sources fully, to keep clear operating goals in mind, or to consider long-term implications and to respond to popular needs, wants and values.[7]

Burns was critical of the practical advice of Machiavelli to rulers, which dramatizes the half truth that humans are selfish and therefore can be best manipulated in appeals to their selfishness. This strategy fails to recognize that appeals to the best in people may be stronger than manipulation. By the same token, he questioned Max Weber's preference for the "ethic of responsibility," in which ideals are trimmed to practicalities, in contrast to the "ethic of ultimate ends," in which ideals are pursued even if they are illusions. Burns depicted the ethic of responsibility as permitting actions that are expedient, opportunist, and self-serving, all masquerading as the practical. Burns would reformulate the ethic of responsibility to admit the consideration of long-term goals. But, of course, Weber did just this. Burns may have failed to appreciate that a transformational politician cannot be an effective transforming leader without having mastered and practiced transactional politics. There is no corresponding requirement for the transactional politician. Abraham Lincoln was practicing transactional politics when he ran for the presidency on the cause of saving the Union, even if slavery in the South had to be tolerated, although not extended. He was a transactional politician when he freed the southern slaves in the Emancipation Proclamation without disturbing slavery in the five border states that had stayed in the Union. He reached for transforming possibilities in the Gettysburg Address when he undertook to reformulate the moral purpose of the American Union, to shift it from a federal union of states to a government of, by, and for the people, with liberty for all. But Lincoln never ceased being a clever transactional leader.

Burns argued that all politicians must make moral choices. They have to do more than just protect their reputations, choices, and resources because, if they do only this, they unduly may limit their goals. Neustadt would reply, of course, that a lofty purpose is useless if it is not served by skillful politics. But Neustadt did not consider that the articulation of purpose may be the best political strategy. As Burns put it: "Clearly the leader who commands compelling causes has an extraordinary personal influence over followers."[8]

Neustadt and Burns understood presidential leadership of public opinion quite differently. Neustadt counseled presidents to teach the public about policies in relation to events and conditions that impinge on people's lives. This, of course, can be given a narrow or a broad interpretation. Teaching citizens to accept the need for a tax increase speaks directly to concrete conditions of life and tangible stakes. But Roosevelt's using the fall of France in 1940 to persuade the public and Congress to support aid to Britain illustrates a more diffuse sense of the public good.

Burns reached high and asked politicians to articulate shared moral purposes to citizens, often with the deliberate intent of awakening latent needs and values that would be recognized and accepted once confronted. This is not Neustadt's appeal to enlightened self-interest, but the awakening of collective commitments. For Burns, leadership is nothing "if not linked to collective purposes."[9] Politicians of the best sort do not so much represent citizens as decide what challenges they will present to the public.

Burns depicted Franklin Roosevelt as a classic transactional leader who was ultimately a prisoner of the pluralist politics of stasis. He could carry the New Deal no farther in a progressive direction or fashion an ideological realignment of the two parties. Neustadt made no such demands on FDR. Indeed, Roosevelt may have been the very model of a democratic politician who pursues the ethic of ultimate ends in the most general way but also tests each step that he takes according to the ethic of responsibility. Perhaps this is the most that can be asked of a Roosevelt or a Lincoln in a pluralist democracy.

William Riker has offered a third conception of leadership: the deliberate attempt to structure political situations so that opponents will either have to submit or be trapped. There is also the possibility of redefining conventional political conflicts to permit new coalitions to be created. Riker referred to his strategy as heresthetics, the science of manipulation and strategy of winning. It is different from rhetoric, which is persuasion on the merits of a case. For Riker, the "politically rational man is the man who would rather win than lose, regardless of the particular stakes." A rational act is the best choice from the set of possibilities that will enable one to win. A leader must understand the goals and incentives of others to move them. And such strategies will work because "when reasonable people who have the same goals are placed in similar situations they behave similarly."[10] Riker's example of clever heresthetics is Lincoln's challenge to Stephen Douglas, the incumbent Democratic senator from Illinois, in their 1858 debates.[11] Lincoln asked Douglas if it was possible for the legislature of a territory to exclude slavery from that territory by law before the territory became a state. He thus placed Douglas on the horns of a dilemma. If he answered yes, he would please his northern Democratic supporters. But he would risk offending potential southern Democratic supporters in the presidential nomination contest and subsequent election campaign in 1860 should he be the nominee of the national Democratic party. Douglas answered yes and won reelection to the Senate. But in so doing, he took the first step toward dividing the Democratic party over slavery, and thus contributed to his own later defeat as the candidate of a northern rump Democratic party. According to Riker, Lincoln was preparing the way for his strategy of winning a Republican plurality in the presidential election of 1860 by dividing the Democrats over slavery.

The heresthetician does not create preferences, but continually probes the political possibilities to find some way to redirect the preferences of others. Lincoln is said by Riker to have astutely seen how he might unite his own party and divide his opponents. Such calculated opportunism may introduce important shifts in the structure of politics, as it was in 1860.

In the judgment of historians, Riker's analysis is accurate but incomplete.[12] The positions of both Lincoln and Douglas on the question posed were known before the debates. Douglas had publicly stated that a territorial legislature need not act at all if it wanted to exclude slavery from the territory. Lincoln's question was less a trap, although it was so used, than a form of making clear his opposition to the spread of slavery on moral grounds. The Union must be saved by confining slavery to the Old South, in the hope that it eventually would erode there. Douglas did not think it possible to save the Union by containing slavery. He saw Lincoln's policy as dooming the United States. The fundamental difference between Lincoln and Douglas was that Douglas denied the common humanity of blacks and whites, and

Lincoln affirmed it. Douglas was willing to keep the country together by any possible means. Lincoln did not agree because he regarded slavery as immoral, even though the Constitution permitted it in the South. Lincoln's approach provides a classic illustration of the American dilemma about race. He believed in the common humanity of whites and blacks, but accepted the practices of inequality. Values conflicted in Lincoln's uncertainty, but in his political leadership he moved the country in the direction of equality, no matter how painful or slow.

It was Lincoln's achievement to present this dilemma in terms with which the average American could identify, and it reflected an authenticity that touched Americans more deeply than either abolitionists' rhetoric or Douglas's dismissal of the principle of human equality. Purpose set strategy for both of these politicians. Certainly, Riker captured Lincoln's political cleverness in devising a heresthetic maneuver. But such a strategy was quite subordinate to a larger purpose that was far more important in Lincoln's eventual election to the presidency.

These three distinct, valuable, and overlapping understandings of political leadership cover the range of the resources on which politicians draw as they seek to lead. Leaders may construct bargaining coalitions, engage in strategic maneuvers to outflank their rivals, and use rhetoric to inspire and persuade. Some politicians may use all three strategies simultaneously. However, the closer a leader is to bargaining as a strategy within a stable system of politics, the less likely he is to turn to rhetoric for help. Rhetoric is necessary when times are uncertain and citizens are anxious for articulation of troubling problems and dilemmas. Both bargaining and rhetoric may be joined to heresthetic maneuvers. But heresthetics is most likely to be effective in fluid rather than static conditions and is therefore quite compatible with rhetoric, as strategy rather than substance.

Each of these three strategies of leadership has the potential for greater and lesser degrees of persuasion or control. A may approach B with a bargain from which both benefit, or A may force B to accept a bargain to his disadvantage because A has greater political resources. Yet B cannot just be swept aside. A may convince B that a certain action is the morally correct thing to do, or A may so agitate B's followers against B's position that B, lacking a politically effective reply, is intimidated from fighting back. Finally, through heresthetic strategies A may fashion a new coalition, each of whose constituents has an eye to his own advantage. Such a coalition, lacking a foundation in persuasion, may be inherently unstable because based on control. These are the first building blocks of our conceptions of skill and strategy: bargaining, maneuver, and rhetoric, each partaking of persuasion and control.

However, these strategies are rudderless without the faculty of discernment, the ability to estimate, more or less accurately, the kinds of political action that will be successful in a given historical context. Discernment is the master skill because politicians must use the lesser skills in a larger strategy of discernment that will guide their actions. Each president must bring to his administration such a strategic view of purposes that takes into account what he judges to be feasible. If that strategy is well matched to the historical context, then bargaining, heresthetics, and rhetoric, when used appropriately, will be effective.

Character

It is not a familiar idea to students of leadership but it is an obvious fact of everyday life that people may follow leaders because they trust their integrity, judgment, and competence. The hope and inspiration that leaders exude are contagious. Political leaders who are comfortable with themselves appear to be self-confident, and affairs can be safely left in their hands. Such leaders are emotionally secure enough to reach out for ideas without defensiveness. Emotionally insecure leaders, who may be unable to listen and learn, but who resort to defensiveness, will inspire anything but confidence. They may effectively appeal to the insecurities of others, however. Character, in the sense of the way people organize their approach to themselves and others, is a potential skill in the persuasion of others. Leaders who exhibit intellectual and emotional security, when joined to other political skills, are likely to rely on strategies of persuasion rather than control, just as insecure politicians may take refuge in manipulation.

Persuasion, in all the guises already presented, is a far more effective approach to leadership than control, because persuasion is based on willing assent. Trickery is slippery and is not the stuff of enduring coalitions. Attempts to lead by control will therefore prove unsuccessful, since those subject to force will fight back. Of course, some control is always present in persuasion, and some persuasion is always present in strategies of control.

The Individual Leader in History: Skill in Context

The political resources available to American presidents change across time. Skill and the will to act are always important, but as Glendower says to Hotspur in *Henry IV*, Part 1: "I can call spirits from the vasty deep." And Hotspur replies,

> Why, so can I, or so can any man;
> But will they come when you do call for them?[13]

Skill is reinforced by favorable political contexts and is disadvantaged in unfavorable contexts. Stephen Skowronek has attempted to understand presidential leadership according to the political regimes that some presidents create and in which others must work. He traced the construction and destruction of partisan coalitions throughout American history.[14] Four presidents of Reconstruction—Thomas Jefferson, Andrew Jackson, Abraham Lincoln, and Franklin Roosevelt—challenged the foundations of the previous political regimes and built new coalitions to take their place. These administrations are inevitably challenged and give way in turn. Three other kinds of presidents worked within each regime. Presidents of Articulation—such as Theodore Roosevelt and Lyndon Johnson—provide vigorous leadership to carry out the unfinished but promised agenda of the period of Reconstruction. Presidents of Preemption—Grover Cleveland, Woodrow Wilson, and Dwight Eisenhower—succeed only briefly in overturning the majority coalition, usually because of some deep conflict within it. Finally, presidents of Disjunction—John Quincy Adams, James Buchanan, Herbert Hoover, and Jimmy Carter—serve at the concluding years of a once dominant regime and are vulnerable to the challenges of an alternative coalition.

Skowronek did not explicitly explore the repertoire of skills and strategies required for each type of presidency. It would appear that bargaining, maneuver, and rhetoric have their places. But the most valuable faculty is presidents' perceptiveness about the political context in which they find themselves. They must see the possibilities of political action in their time, whether it is to create, invigorate, or preserve a regime. Presidents must "situate themselves in public discourse" in order to "preempt the authority of others."

Skowronek thus outlined a dynamic framework of structure and agency. A president is deemed successful if he has exploited fully the possible resources for political leadership in his historical context. No one president can be an exemplar for all the others. Eisenhower was perhaps very shrewd to recognize that his presidency of Preemption would be most effective by taking a nonpartisan stance above politics. Carter and Clinton may have failed to fully understand that it was a mistake to propose ambitious legislative programs during periods marked by a fragmented Democratic coalition and public distrust of government. Skowronek's most successful presidents are those of Reconstruction and Articulation. Their talents are reinforced by popular politics, which they know how to exploit. Skowronek stayed close to his historical schema and did not venture into larger questions of the role of individual politicians in historical stability, change, and consolidation as a general theoretical question. But he has shown convincingly that all presidents may be usefully compared when the categories of comparison encompass the political work that all presidents must do.

Ahistorical approaches to understanding presidential leadership fail because they cannot capture the variety of the past. Those in the progressive tradition who see the presidency as the sole source of energy in national government can only despair that such energy appears in a dramatic way so seldom. And then they must explain when and how presidential power is sometimes abused. The struggle with this problem has led many progressives to search for quasi-parlimentary ways to strengthen executive leadership, through party reform or constitutional amendment. Critics of this president-centered approach regard it as myopic and describe national government as a balancing act between the "tandem institutions" of presidency and Congress, in which policy initiatives come from many possible sources and action is undertaken through cooperation, even in the form of political maneuver and conflict.[15] These revisionists challenge the ideal and reality of the president-centered approach. Neither ideal nor reality is necessary for effective government. Each approach understands something that the other does not. Times of national crisis and challenge may very well require bold presidential leadership of Congress. And yet year in and year out, Congress and president, working together, do seem to face and resolve many problems.

The long-term historical model of Skowronek is superior to either ahistorical approach in capturing the variety of recurring leadership situations. He also considered important aspects of presidential leadership that go beyond the question of legislative achievement, which is the only test for both the presidentialists and their critics. This preoccupation reflects the long-standing concern about whether institutional checks and balances work well and avoid paralysis of government. But although Skowronek analyzed the political work of presidents in constructing and managing partisan regimes, he did not look at the presidents themselves and consider the possible effects of their styles of leadership on the quality of political life.

❖ ❖ ❖

CULTURAL LEADERSHIP

The chief task of political leadership is to present effective and politically appealing remedies for public problems. This is not an easy combination. Policy experts, advocates, and citizens will adhere to "rational" solutions, whether scientific, moral, or representational. The wise politician must acknowledge their claims, but also convince them to accept the imperfections of politics. It is just a step from that wise discernment to an unjustified conclusion that the politician knows best because others are too naive to understand what must be done. This is a line the intellectually and morally honest politician must not cross because to do so is to abandon the primary responsibility of political leadership—to combine purpose and politics. Abraham Lincoln was neither a pure rationalist nor a moral absolutist, and yet he used politics to teach deep moral truths. Cultural leadership is the only way by which politicians may appeal to "the better angels of our nature." Political culture is historical, contextual, and dynamic. It changes over time. All action for the future is guided, in part, by the cultural resources provided by the past. Of course, culture in a complex polity is not monolithic, and recurring contradictions may be a cultural theme. We are known by our conflicts. The acceptance and exercise of political power are very sensitive to cultural nuances. Culture is not simply a distribution of attitudes among all the members of a population, but a manifestation of human imagination, which is the first step toward creativity. Culture gives emotional life to tradition and may provide flexibility to what is believed to be possible. It grows from historical events that produce stories shared in collective memory. The polity is understood in terms of successful and unsuccessful plots of ongoing stories of general importance. The writing of the Declaration of Independence and the Constitution, Lincoln's emancipation of the slaves, Wilson's support of the League of Nations to prevent war, Franklin Roosevelt's courage in crisis—these are all cultural stories. Politicians use these stories and create new ones of their own as particular problems are faced and resolved. Political culture thus develops through continual adaptation in ways that are understood only in retrospect. The anchored character of culture provides both change and continuity.

Max Weber regarded beliefs and conventions as the legacies of past struggles about the proper character of a society.[16] He rejected historical materialism in favor of the "inexhaustible complexity of causal pluralism." He saw social life as a congeries of values in conflict. Historical interpretation and reinterpretation thus never stop. This view of historical processes as both structured and malleable received grand expression in the thought of John Dewey, who believed that society and politics are neither bound by complete necessity nor subject to compete randomness. There is latitude for human creativity, and the freedom to act according to moral purposes is the essence of humanity.[17] Thus ideas in history are both intellectual and contextual. Weber cited "elective affinity" in which ideas and social institutions are congruent. If ideas are to take root as resources for social action, they must express the felt necessities of people's lives and must be in harmony with political and social structures. The pure idealist and pure materialist are naive. But there is no guarantee that ideas and material conditions will always come together constructively. That is the task of leadership, and leaders may fail. However, neither success nor failure can be fully explained by the latent congruence of ideas and conditions; the creativity and energy that leaders bring to the task of joining them is also important. The wild card of leadership paradoxically inhibits the development of generalizations about leadership in history because of the very uncertainty of whether the wild card will be played.

In his depiction of the polity as a community and of politics as the means for the definition of the purposes of the community, Aristotle regarded politicians as less the advocates for interests than the leaders of coalitions that unite interests according to overriding beliefs and values. He did not deny the power of group self-interest, but asked statesmen to control and direct interests by explaining what all citizens held in common. This was the only way to transcend the politics of manipulation and divisiveness for Aristotle. We become virtuous and just by practicing virtue and justice, and the practice of politics, at its best, is an exercise in the definition of justice.[18] By the same token, the appeals of politicians to the dark side of human nature—fear, anger, prejudice, anger—even though disguised as policy ideas, may be made attractive to a large variety of citizens. But dark appeals are unlikely to work politically if the human values on which the democratic polity is based are widespread and robust. Machiavelli was right. The virtue of citizens is the best guarantor of a republic.

The Buddhist saying that "if the string is too tight it will snap, but if it is too loose, the instrument will not play" offers a metaphor for the importance of balancing purpose and prudence. Politicians must work within the opportunities for and boundaries on action set by their culture. Again, they must be guided by discernment—the faculty for recognizing the attainable balance of purpose and prudence for political action. Of course, politicians must make such judgments, and history may prove them right or wrong. But it is difficult for historians to determine whether policies that were not attempted might have been achieved. Nor can a politician know with certainty whether a bold step will work unless he takes it. Discernment would thus seem to be a synonym for prudence. I do not wish to say this. Rather, I ask that discernment temper purpose with prudence so that action is realistic and does not overreach. But how can one know this, either at the time of action, or later, except in cases of clear-cut success or failure? The best answer I can give is to ask the politician and the observer to try to understand the culture of the polity well enough to make reasoned judgments about what is or was possible in a given context. It was eventually clear to Franklin Roosevelt, and to subsequent observers, that American political parties could not be realigned along liberal–conservative lines, given the structure and culture of American politics. It was also clear after 1936 that the American system of free enterprise would not give way to any kind of national economic planning. Does this mean that the National Recovery Administration of Roosevelt's first term was a naive conception? The answer is yes, but it was not conceived as national planning and it soon became clear that the tensions between business and labor undermined the NRA plan.

Discernment does not require the politician to read the future, which no one can do, but only to have a good sense of the possibilities in a given situation. It is easy to recognize the substitution of ideological aspiration and unreality for empirical calculation, as in Clinton's misadventure in health-care reform in 1995. There was a burst of enthusiasm for reform, but careful political soundings might have revealed the limits on action. Prudence should have guided purpose. Each president must set a broad strategy, across the policy board, for his presidency, and the perceptiveness of his discernment will be the success or undoing of his presidency. Clinton sought to learn from the mistakes of the Carter presidency, but then proceeded to repeat two of them: hiring an inexperienced White House staff and proposing a grandiose legislative program. It is fair to call these two presidents' errors failures of discernment.

❖ ❖ ❖

TEACHING REALITY

Politicians must try their best to describe the world and their plans for dealing with it in the most accurate terms they can muster. In short, they must teach reality. It is a matter of honesty, but good intentions do not guarantee an accurate reading of circumstances. And one person's reality is not necessarily another's. Few economists thought that the supply-side theory of taxation and economic growth supported valid and responsible policies and were happy to point out that the federal deficits that emerged and grew during the Reagan administration were in part a result of that theory. But Reagan never abandoned it. Can we say that he was refusing to teach reality? Many would say so, but it could also be argued that he was preaching hope that the economy would rebound as a result of his policies, which it did, and that this was teaching reality as well. Reality is thus very elusive. But politicians and their critics, including the historians who ultimately judge politicians, are continually in search of empirical reality. They assume that the more closely policies match empirical reality, the more likely are the theories implicit in those policies to work.

The murkiness of this subject suggests that it is prudent to fall back on secondary criteria to assess the teaching of reality. Does a politician contribute to the quality of political discourse in the polity? Political rhetoric may have to be simplified, but that is not the same as distortion. Therefore, it is fair to ask if the rhetoric is informative and concrete, recognizes contingencies and uncertainties, and appears generally designed to educate. Franklin Roosevelt's fireside chats on the radio illustrate such speech at its best. He described the problem to be addressed concretely, explained the common sense of the proposed solution, and admitted uncertainties that could be faced in the future. The chats were designed to educate rather than manipulate. This kind of speech is in contrast to rhetoric that uses stereotypes and scapegoats, provides limited information, and is dogmatic and rigid. One criterion of such language is its diversion of attention away from particular policy ideas to the appeal to abstract creeds, which are not substitutes for carefully explained policies. Such crude political rhetoric, which aims to mislead the audience by the distortion of facts, will be sufficient to detect the demagogue, along with others who do not deliberately seek to mislead but do not raise the quality of democratic discourse.

The politician's primary criterion for teaching reality, though, must be his audience's assessment of the validity of his message. The closer rhetoric is to the actual historical situation, the more likely it is a reliable guide to action.

Teaching reality in politics naturally relies on the politician's faculty of discernment in the effort to articulate plausible remedies for emerging policy problems that will win general political support. Politicians cannot consult prophets who can tell the future, and they are not Hegelian supermen who know that history is moving in a given direction and can will us that way. They are merely humans who must make choices. For example, something must be done about the degradation of the environment by pollution. We all know that by now, but there are many different solutions. And to return to an earlier example: Was Reagan teaching reality when he persisted with his policies based on supply-side economics, which did not live up to its promise? Every empirical check revealed the limitation of the theory. The fact that the voters rejected the theory's claims when Robert Dole made them as a presidential candidate in 1996 strengthens my point. Those who teach reality are offering their subjective interpretations, but because they must be shared and assessed, they can be refined. And this is the task of competitive politics. We certainly fumble collectively into the future. No one ever fully understands the society in which he or she lives. But the politician who can articulate widely shared concerns about emerging problems and recommend plausible policies to address those concerns is a step ahead of other politicians.

My formulation is certainly an idealistic one. It assumes, or hopes, that politicians will try to teach reality as best they can. This argument is properly challenged by a contrary view, derived from Machiavelli, that political leaders will fail if they try to teach reality and would do much better if they tailored their rhetoric to the prejudices of followers, not just because it may be easier to pander, but because citizens fear reality. The critique of the realist cannot simply be dismissed. At the very least, it raises the question of whether democratic discourse, even that of the highest quality, must rely on crude simplification, partial distortion, and selective use of information if anyone is to govern at all. I simply pose this hard question here and hope that it can be answered as we move along.

Another aspect of teaching reality is preaching. People often must be exhorted to stand up for the values in which they believe and which transend prudence. A committed politician will reach farther, using moral preaching to appeal to citizens' "better angels"; for example, Lyndon Johnson, on behalf of his antipoverty program, urged citizens to "do something you can be proud of." If such preaching is to be effective, it must be couched in politically appealing language that takes account of what people can be expected to support. Of course, preaching may create a new, shared sense of purpose and thereby change what is possible politically. James MacGregor Burns argued that leadership, in his definition, must be linked to "collective purposes" that express "the needs, aspirations, and values of followers."[19] Thus dominance and control without persuasion are not legitimate acts of leadership. The search for political power as such, which meets the desires of only the powerful, rather than the needs of followers, is not leadership. Thus to Burns, Hitler and Stalin were not leaders, in the normative definition he gives the term. He then complicated the matter by asking leaders to "make conscious what lies unconscious among followers." But surely Hitler did this in his rise to power and even afterward when his popularity in Germany was very great. Was not Hitler expressing collective purpose? Burns would logically have to admit yes, but then he shifted his ground and argued that "at the highest level of moral development persons are guided by near universal ethical principles of human rights and respect for individual dignity."[20] This additional idea permits us to separate genuine leaders like Roosevelt from demagogues like Hitler; the first led in the direction of human fulfillment, while the second led into a demonic world that violated the best of human nature.

Even those who are less than certain that universal moral norms may prevail in politics cannot avoid the responsibility for moral appraisal in their judgment of political leaders. Teaching reality, in this normative sense, is teaching what one understands to be moral truths. There is plenty of room for disagreement in a polity about the degree of moral consensus required as the foundation of the polity itself. At this point, I do not wish to consider whether there can be a public interest for all citizens or simply a set of compromises among citizens with competing moral views about how to live together. I will return to this question in the final chapter. I show my hand, however, when I insist that it is incumbent on politicians to evoke what are believed to be the moral aspirations with which the very identity of the polity is interwoven. Either the American polity is about the achievement of equality of opportunity, in diverse forms, for all its citizens, or it is no longer what we believed the best of the American polity to have been.

Competitive politics is necessarily a politics of cultural interpretation. Politicians who appeal to the dark side of American traditions, such as racism and hyperpatriotism, must compete in the political marketplace. They are not likely to prevail with great numbers of people as long as there is widespread belief in the values that are central to American traditions. If they do prevail, then the polity is no longer what it was.

Politicians may also fail to teach reality because they and their followers in the public have fallen into "cultural traps" of illusion about the kinds of problems facing the society. All polities carry such traps in their political cultures. The shock of defeat in Vietnam may have been necessary to persuade American leaders to seriously question the validity of the commitment to counter "aggression" everywhere, which became the credo of the Cold War. The American resistance to the necessities of some aspects of the welfare state may be both realistic and illusory in its insistence that self-help will be possible despite the inability of the economy to create jobs for everyone. Such traps may never be overcome, and so politicians will have to accept illusion as a continuing part of politics. The illusions of grandiosity and hubris, as evident in foreign policy, may possibly be corrected as they collide with reality. Conversely, realistic strategies of action may be unable to prevail, at least in the short run, because of the strength of cultural traps.

The political benefits and penalties of teaching reality in the short run are unclear because electorates often do not listen to urgings, warnings, and appeals to confront unpleasant facts or new, unperceived realities. One may accept this fact of political life and yet recognize that ultimately wise counsel may prevail, except when cultural traps are incredibly strong. But skill in telling the truth in the short run may contribute to the success of the attempt to teach reality.

❖ ❖ ❖

A MODEL OF POLITICAL LEADERSHIP

The leading ideas in this chapter are shown in the table on page 46. This model is more than a checklist of possibly interconnected variables and less than a causal theory. A model can be a theory at rest, with the relations left unstated. I have constructed the model to capture the political possibilities set forth in this chapter. There is an implicit causal theory that may be empirically tested. Skill and strategy work most effectively when they are congruent with the possibilities in the political context. And particular skills are most effective when they are matched to the tasks for which they are required. Persuasion is superior to control because it is based on confirmed assent. Character is a skill insofar as it influences the credibility of a leader.

Strategy and skill in context	*Persuasion/control*
Discernment	Bargaining
Character	Heresthetics
Psychological health	Rhetoric
Moral commitment	
Integrity	
Cultural leadership	
Purpose	
Prudence	
Discernment	
Teaching reality (or illusion)	
Teaching	
Preaching	
Demagogy	
Cultural traps	
Short-run or long-run	
politics and policy	

Psychological health, moral commitment, and personal integrity, which lend themselves more to persuasion than to control, are the hallmarks of a confident and successful leader.

The most important task of political leadership is cultural interpretation, which is best achieved by using discernment to balance purpose and prudence in ways that match the possibilities in the political context. Popular leaders may be effective in denying emerging historical realities in the short run, but such denials are much less likely to work in the long run. Politicians who eschew transformational politics in favor of simple transactional politics will help to make politics work but not to achieve the deepest aspirations of the culture. Teaching reality is therefore the effort to evoke such aspirations in a manner that tells the truth about the practical steps needed to fulfill them.

These propositions could be cast as utilitarian by claiming that honesty is the best policy because it works. This may be true, but it does not exhaust my thought. Persuasion, conducted with honesty, is a value that is not automatically achieved but must be worked for.

Skill, which takes practice to perfect, must be driven by the moral desire to persuade, rather than control. Cultural leadership is more than simply mouthing conventional wisdom and, while served by technique, cannot be induced by technical proficiency. The leader must care enough to make the effort; there must be an infusion of will with art. And, finally, teaching reality, while it relies on virtuosity to connect words and deeds, requires commitment to be effective. The utilitarian propositions about what works will, in fact, not work unless driven by strong normative purposes.

A realist who follows Machiavelli may claim that control must be used if authority is not to be lost. Persuasion has its limits. Character, at least in the form of integrity, is a handicap for political leadership. A political leader who aims to be good is naive, for his rivals are ready to take advantage of his goodness. Discernment is thus put to different purposes in this dark approach to politics. It is necessary to practice the arts of the demagogue in order to prevail in politics and keep the polity afloat. Indeed, it is irresponsible to do otherwise. One cannot have a politics of saints.

Leadership by control, appealing to the dark side of culture and teaching illusion, also requires great commitment and artistry. Hitler was an artist, but his techniques, although well developed, were driven by his demonic purposes. The parallel with persuasion, appeal to the angels of our better nature, and teaching reality is clear. Energetic, talented leadership is required both to persuade and to control.

The remainder of this book will explore these ideas in both empirical and normative terms in the hopes of freeing the study of political leadership from excessive preoccupation with power and its uses, in favor of an understanding of political leadership as moral agency. Since the central task of political leadership is cultural interpretation, we now turn to an analysis of American political culture.

3

Cultural Leadership

❖ ❖ ❖ ❖ ❖ ❖ ❖ ❖ ❖ ❖ ❖ ❖ ❖ ❖ ❖

The two American political traditions that are explored in Chapter 2 in political terms can also be understood in constitutional language. The first is the regime with the three branches of government held in equipoise by constitutional checks and balances set out in a written document. Each branch is understood to be representative of the people, who are sovereign.[1] But there is also the extraconstitutional idea of government focused on the presidency, which James S. Young has called a "leadership regime."[2]

James MacGregor Burns contended that American political history never developed a normative conception of the place of leadership in American democracy because of the strength of the democratic myth that the people are sovereign. The people are represented by institutions rather than leaders. Young approached the same question from the other end and observed that American "political discourse disconnects the idea of leadership from being led."[3] Thus we have followers without leaders and leaders without followers.

The constitutional tradition of balance does not require a theory of leadership. The processes of government are so widespread and participatory, and the institutions so permeable, that the idea of the people as sovereign, working through representative institutions, is sufficient. This seems to be the way that publics over the years think of Congress, as a representative institution and balance wheel for policy making. However, this idea can cause frustration and a credibility gap between what government does and what citizens think they want. This frustration is inherent in the constitutional model because the political incentives of politicians in such a system push them toward representation rather than governance, with a resulting clash of many different agendas. Thus legislative politicians are boosted as representatives of factions and then derided because Congress as a whole appears to be leaderless. This may help explain why voters admire their own member of Congress, who represents them, and disapprove of the seeming circus of Congress as a body.

The supposed shortcomings of this model explains why we have had leadership regimes, particularly in times of national challenge. But there is popular ambivalence about such regimes because of the strength of the constitutional model in our belief system and the absence of a theory of how leaders are supposed to connect with followers in a leadership regime.

In the twentieth century, conservative political ideology has blessed the constitutional model and condemned presidential leadership regimes, which progressives have supported as the key to energetic government. But with the presidencies of Richard Nixon and Ronald Reagan, conservatives accepted the legitimacy of leadership regimes, as long as the presidents were conservative. Presidential power was to be used to halt the proliferation of government programs. Progressive ideology did not fully revert to a defense of the constitutional model because its conception of government requires executive leadership. So both conservative and progressive leadership regimes have found themselves at odds with congressional politicians of both camps. The problem for leadership regimes is that they lack the influence over the other branches of government to prevail except during brief periods of political empowerment.

These institutional disconnects are analogous to and reinforced by the deep uncertainties in the American polity about the purposes and proper extent of government. Policy conflicts and deadlocks between president and Congress reflect uncertainty about what government should be doing, and conflicting conceptions of institutional authority further complicate matters. These tensions between competing conceptions of government are evident within leadership regimes, as the political ups and downs of the Roosevelt, Johnson, and Reagan presidencies reveal.

Americans have been willing to empower presidents in times of national challenge, but the empowerment is tentative and temporary. Thus presidents with ambitious legislative programs may assess their expectations of success in two ways: estimate both the degree of acceptability of policy ideas and the degree of personal influence that they may exercise in legislative policy making. This insight was the basis for Richard Neustadt's proposition that the best guide for the viability of a president's policy is his own sense of potential influence with other actors in the system.[4]

The greatest potential resource for presidents, then, as they seek to lead in a fragmented institutional world, was explained by the historian Dixon Wecter. They must "hitch the great bandwagon to the star of American idealism."[5] When they do so, they draw on a prophetic tradition that, although derived from the Bible, is part of American political culture. Mark Roelofs posited the "Kingly Model" of the Hebrew Bible as the foundation of the American prophetic impulse.[6] Moses, David, and Joshua led their people according to a tradition of leadership that used prophetic language to evoke concrete historical experiences through narrative stories about the collective life of their people, not only in the past but for the future. These leaders appealed to a common history and a common life and declared to the people the choices they must make.

This tradition has worked in American civil religion as presidents have used narrative to tell a national story, invoke national ideals, and state crucial choices. Abraham Lincoln did this at Gettysburg and in his second inaugural address. His language was biblical in its prophetic tone. He told Americans that they are a people with a higher calling and asked them to resume their fundamental national identity. Twentieth-century presidents have continually reminded the nation of its early covenant and purpose. It is inconceivable that a Canadian or a British prime minister would lead with such language.

The great frustration of leadership in the presidency, however, is that prophetic rhetoric, while a great resource, is seldom sufficient by itself to achieve presidential purposes. The presidential office is caught between transactional and transformational politics.

❖ ❖ ❖

AMERICAN POLITICAL CULTURE

In order to understand the cultural resources available to presidents and the cultural restraints on their actions, we must consider the broad themes of American political culture. Do they help explain what politicians are able to do? Do politicians invoke cultural resources, and are they constrained by the outer limits on belief and practice set by culture? A delineation of political culture is thus a vehicle for the interpretation of presidential actions. The best point of departure is the work of Louis Hartz, who provided the classic statement to which subsequent discourse has responded. Hartz's central insight is that American "individualism" sets the terms for all American politics. The ideal of a society of free individuals who compete in every sphere of life precludes any theory of government and society based either on inequality as a principle or on radical egalitarianism. Just as John Locke once wrote in reference to the state of nature that "all the world was America," so the "liberalism" of Locke became the guiding star of the American experience. There was no place for Tory or Leveler.[7]

The virgin environment of the New World, with its seemingly endless frontier, guaranteed the "elective affinity" of setting and beliefs. The central contest of American politics has been between two kinds of individualism. Economic individualism embraces the doctrines of capitalism. The purpose of government is to protect the creativity of entrepreneurs and markets, which leads to well-being. Democratic individualism appeals to government to redress the social inequalities that result from economic individualism. In neither case is the validity of individualism denied. The protagonists wear different clothes across time as the Federalists give way to the Whigs and then to the Republicans. And the limited-government ideas of the Jeffersonians and Jacksonians are transformed into the reform ideas of the progressives and New Dealers in which government is used to curb and reform capitalism according to new principles of democratic individualism. The master assumption of American political thought is "the reality of atomistic social freedom."[8] The two national interpretations of individualism have been characters in a political drama in which each part has needed the other for the play to continue.

The achievement of Whig politics was to adapt the capitalistic ethic of Alexander Hamilton to a creed in which all Americans could share in the capitalist dream. The belief in social and economic mobility for individuals dramatized in the Horatio Alger stories, in which poor boys rise to fortune by their merits, also appealed to Thomas Jefferson's desire for equal opportunity in the pursuit of happiness. The progressive and New Deal reformers preached the need to curb private economic power in order to foster the Horatio Alger theme for all people. Capitalism was to be reformed so that it would work better. The Great Society of Lyndon Johnson was in this progressive tradition; for example, the war on poverty was presented as a gigantic exercise in self-help. American progressives must always prove their commitment to capitalism, and thus socialist ideas have no place in our politics. By the same token, self-styled conservatives dare not deny that their scheme of things will improve the lives of ordinary people.

Hartz was critical of interpretations of American political history as a form of class warfare. But he also denied the "pluralist" view that all politics can be explained by conflicts among interests within a shared ideology. He regarded our politics as being about competing interpretations of the American dream of "liberty and justice for all." The central debate is about the role of government in achieving that dream. And the political winners change across time as the central problems appear to be either to promote capitalism or to reform it. Each set of legitimate values has been invoked selectively as the politics of the time provided the opportunity.

Hartz extended his thesis to explain American isolationism and interventionism abroad as two sides of the same cultural coin. Herbert Hoover returned from the Versailles peace conference of 1919 disillusioned with power politics and subsequently advocated American detachment from the corruption of realpolitik. Woodrow Wilson preached, at Versailles and to the American people, the message that the ideal of the United States as the beacon of democracy should be extended to all nations. Both men saw America as pure. Both isolationism from and engagement with the rest of the world were derived from America's unique history as a special nation with a high mission. Hartz did not foresee the tragedy of the Vietnam War, in which the idealism of intervention would turn to ashes. But he understood that the driving power of the American dream might become demonic.

Hartz was unhappy with his model of the political culture of the United States. He saw Americans as imprisoned by the celebration of individualism, which cannot be transcended. It is not possible to learn from our mistakes because our mental worlds are bounded. Subsequent critics have questioned his model and challenged the view that it cannot be transcended, and others have leaped to his defense.

Richard Ellis broadened Hartz's framework by adding radical egalitarian and hierarchical strands, each of which has repeatedly challenged the ethos and politics of individualism. It is true that the egalitarian attacks on individualism have not embraced collectivism, but they have preached collective purpose against individualism. The New England Puritans understood individualism only within community, as have the social movements of abolitionism, agrarian populism, prohibition, civil rights, and feminism, as well as the social gospel and moral majorities within evangelical politics. We do have a politics of creedal passion.[9] Ellis's moral crusaders are made of sterner stuff than Hartz's modest reformers. Whereas the crusaders demand results, the reformers are content with a happy pragmatism of process.

Hartz failed to see the other strand in the American political tradition that Ellis identified. It is the fact and ideal of hierarchy, as embodied in the planters of colonial Virginia, the Federalists of New England, the bosses of political machines, and the capitalist magnates.

Ellis strengthened Hartz's insights by modifying them. His characterizations of individualism, egalitarianism, and hierarchy permit each tradition to set strong limits on government even as they interpret freedom differently. The inability of any of the three traditions to resolve the conflicts among them reveals the power of Hartz's original conception of the central principle of liberalism, a belief in both capitalism and democracy, as setting bounds to what politics can accomplish.

While Ellis focused on radical egalitarianism in opposition to liberal individualism, Rogers Smith argued that Hartz ignored the strong and persistent American traditions of racism, sexual inequality, ethnic prejudice, nativism, and religious intolerance. These are "ascriptive forms of Americanism" that have been in no sense liberal or democratic.[10] Smith contended that ideologies and institutions of inequality have been important in our culture, so that Pat Buchanan and Pat Robertson are authentic Americans just as much as Martin Luther King, Jr., and George McGovern. He denied the necessary dominance of the American liberal creed that liberty and justice must be provided to all as a condition of citizenship.

But Hartz did not believe that all would necessarily come right in the end. He doubted the capacities of liberalism, which is the only hope for reform in American politics. Racism, nativism, sexism, and all kinds of social and economic inequalities are facts of American life. Social movements of stronger fiber than pragmatic liberalism attack them. But the problems themselves can be resolved only by the language and practice of the liberal ideology and polity. The facts of hierarchy and inequality and the ideals of community and equality must, sooner or later, be shaped politically by the rhetoric and practices of liberal individualism. Thus action to enhance equality of opportunity, as in the War on Poverty or civil rights, can win politically as long as the values of individualism are not challenged. Hartz's model of American "liberalism" explains the most essential thing, if not everything.

A different tack is taken by those who see liberal ideals themselves unraveling because liberalism is too narrow a philosophy to permit the resolution of divisive political conflicts. This is because the most grievous public problems are not amenable to "liberal" measures. "Conservatives" deny government the authority required to address problems. Instead, they propose policies that would reduce the role of government in the belief that social and economic problems can be best resolved through the market. "Progressives" offer only palliatives for problems that evade the optimistic hopes they bring to politics. Thus neither the call to reform welfare by making people work nor the hope that job training and day care can erase severe social deficits will be effective.

Richard Merelman has argued that the loosely bound culture of liberalism is unable to regulate political and economic hierarchies and thus has failed to fulfill the democratic promise. All industrial democracies have experienced the decline of collective conscience, but the weakness of liberalism in America presents the worst case.[11] For Merelman, the Puritan sense of the commonweal, the republican tradition of the Founders, and the various reform movements have withered and left only a residual liberalism that lacks the moral force to take on and solve collective problems. One result may be the current popular disaffection with government. It would be ironic if the liberalism that is too weak to cope with real problems is too strong as a popular belief to permit efforts to transcend it. We may be the prisoners of our own myths. We resist a politics that would grant more authority to government, but, at the same time, we condemn the consequences. It is paradoxical that the federal government, which is hobbled in so many ways, has become the target of attack as being too powerful. But Americans must use those scapegoats that are culturally available to them.

There are those who would revive the "republican" tradition in our culture as a possible ground for collective commitment. As Robert Bellah and his colleagues put it: "The tension between self-reliant competitive enterprise and a sense of public solidarity empowered by civic republicans has been the most important unresolved problem in American history."[12] The liberal polity needs "imagination" and "vision" in line with "public virtue," and these values must find public expression. But from where is this virtue to derive?

Two rather bleak depictions of our dilemmas deserve mention in this regard. C. Wright Mills found liberalism to be a bankrupt ideology that American elites are able to live by, but that offers nothing for the great number of people. The rhetoric of liberalism is thus divorced from reality for most of us.[13] Michael Sandel argued that no government has ever found a way to resolve public problems without a theory of the "public interest," which must be something more than the sum of individual preferences. But the rights-based American regime does not easily recognize such a public interest.[14] Twentieth-century liberal reform made its peace with centralized power, but the society and polity have become too loose and vast to permit any kind of cohesive "republican" ideas to prevail. So a procedural liberalism guarantees individual rights in courts and the bureaucracy, but the vitality of political life itself erodes. Government becomes a massive shell of rules.

❖ ❖ ❖

PUBLICS AND ELITES

Studies of American attitudes toward government periodically find that citizens are, as one study put it, "philosophical conservatives" and "operational liberals."[15] Americans subscribe to the creed of limited government, but wish to enjoy the benefits of activist government. It is not so much a contradiction as a balancing act in that we acknowledge the tensions between freedom and equality, but refuse to resolve them permanently. We shift back and forth according to the problem, issues, and political appeals of the time.[16] Most of us have absorbed these key values without feeling the imperative to resolve the tensions between them. But we do limit egalitarianism by our individualist beliefs. Conservatives may not completely ignore equality of opportunity, even as they promote inequality of condition. Progressives must promote equality of opportunity, without seeming to create equality of condition. These are the common cultural values of America's liberal tradition. Opposites are held in tension.

It is not a disparagement of the political sophistication of citizens to point out that they may not have coherent partisan ideologies. This is reserved for political elites and the attentive publics who are responsive to them. But ordinary people are quite clear in their own minds about the values and principles of "classical liberalism" that guide their politics. They can simultaneously be for limited and activist government, individualism and equality of opportunity, self-reliance and welfare for the deserving needy. And these balances are adhered to across time despite short-term shifts in emphasis.[17]

Surveys show that Americans prefer freedom over equality, as compared with Europeans, and that their desire for freedom is reinforced by a commitment to the capitalist value of getting ahead in life.[18] Americans appear to believe in the fundamental equality of all people. Prejudice and racial and ethnic animosity are strong in our collective life, and yet we have had the resilience to assimilate incoming minorities generation after generation. But we do not believe in the equal allocation of wealth. Differences of wealth are regarded, for the most part, as evidence of individual merit, and education is understood to be the engine of social and economic opportunity.

We are children of Emerson in our desire to develop our individuality to the fullest, and of Horatio Alger in our desire to get ahead in society. We embrace both capitalism and democracy. Americans do not so much fall in behind capitalist or democratic banners as support both camps to differing degrees. Those who advocate social reforms are enthusiastic democrats and wary capitalists. Those who value order and stability are enthusiastic capitalists and wary democrats. Debates about the proper role of government invoke the mix of values in this American ethos, in which the balance between capitalism and democracy is continually being adjusted.

❖ ❖ ❖

POLITICAL ERAS

The historians Arthur Schlesinger and his son Arthur Schlesinger, Jr., have developed a theory of cycles of political eras that is logically coherent and amenable to prediction because the causes of the cyclic dialectic are inherent to the process itself. The elder Schlesinger identified the prime mover in American political life as the alternation of periods of concern for the rights of the few and periods responsive to the rights of the many.[19] He dates these eras in a general way, as shown in this table for the first half of the twentieth century.

Liberal periods	*Conservative periods*
1901–1919	1920–1932
Theodore Roosevelt	Warren Harding
William Howard Taft	Calvin Coolidge
Woodrow Wilson	Herbert Hoover
1933–1947	
Franklin Roosevelt	
Harry Truman	

Schlesinger regarded the New Deal as ending in 1947 after the Republicans captured control of both houses of Congress in the 1946 elections. The average length of each period, in both the nineteenth and twentieth centuries, is approximately sixteen years. Schlesinger predicted that the conservative period that began in 1947 would last until 1962 and that the next conservative period would appear around 1978. He was not far off in his forecast of the advent of the Kennedy and Reagan presidencies.

The direction of the cycle is progressive because that was Schlesinger's reading of American history. He did not envision the cycle as a circle returning to the same point, but as a spiral in which new conceptions of liberalism and conservatism develop as new problems emerge. The liberal policies are never reversed, but periodically consolidated. Schlesinger was not precise about what causes the cycle. He could find no correlation with economic conditions or war. He rejected the concept of political generations because demarcation is subjective. Finally, he settled on the insight that the interplay of order and change occurs in all human spheres, including politics. Conservative governments fail to solve new problems and are succeeded by liberal administrations, which eventually burn themselves out. Neither fully satisfies popular hopes. Schlesinger believed that conservatives and liberals are the warp and woof of the American political tradition but he put his money on the progressives.

Arthur Schlesinger, Jr., refined his father's theory and brought it up to 1986.[20] The conservatism of the Eisenhower years was followed by the reform presidencies of John Kennedy and Lyndon Johnson, which then gave way to another conservative period with Richard Nixon and Gerald Ford. He gave Jimmy Carter little credit as a progressive, but regarded him as the precursor of Ronald Reagan and a conservative era. His hope was that a new progressive period would begin in the 1990s. He believed his father to have correctly predicted the politics to come, and Bill Clinton's victory in 1992 would give heart to a progressive unless Clinton were to have Carter's problems.

Schlesinger found his father's use of the terms "liberal" and "conservative" to be too broad and substituted the tensions between capitalism and democracy. The former emphasizes the importance of private interests and the institutions that promote them, such as markets. The latter emphasizes democratic values, such as equality, freedom, the general welfare. He equated the democratic impulse with concern for the "public good." Capitalism and democracy had been historic allies against absolute monarchy and feudal aristocracy, but in modern polities, they are somewhat at odds. But like his father, Schlesinger thought that the democratic impulse is stronger than the capitalist one, and therefore gave a progressive interpretation to American history.

A true cycle is self-generating and cannot be caused by external events. Schlesinger argued that each of the two principles of capitalism and democracy becomes ineffective over time and gives way to the other. These reversals are not inevitable, however. They have to be set in motion by leaders. Here, he revived the theory of generations rejected by his father. Political generations do exist and are created by formative historical events, such as depression and war. Thus the young progressives brought us the New Deal. And the youth of the New Deal created the Great Society. The students of the 1960s now staff the Clinton administration. The young conservatives of the 1950s served in the Nixon administration of the 1970s, and so on. Presidents become the heroes of political generations and articulate their values. Of course, an entire generation cannot be of one political cast. Kennedy and Nixon belonged to the same generation. The symmetry of Schlesinger's schema is a bit too neat, with a new generation coming to power every thirty years. He wanted the cycle to be internally generated, but acknowledged the importance of external events. I suggest that cycles of this kind are not internally generated but are triggered by historical events. The repetition of sequences between progressive and conservative periods occurs because the universe of American politics cannot reach beyond the fundamental "liberal" framework of the political culture. *also "labels" are the same,* *but content differs.*

❖ ❖ ❖

SEQUENCES OF POLITICS AND POLICY

A rough pattern of sequences of "conservative" and "progressive" presidencies in twentieth-century American politics is evident. They appear to be both animated and bounded by the fundamental American belief in and values of "liberalism." Presidents elected to achieve a pause in government fail to address new problems, and opponents win the presidency. Those presidents carry out reform programs as a result of their election, but the programs inevitably meet with opposition and a call for stability and a period of consolidation. Critics of this pattern of politics argue that neither conservative nor progressive administrations address "real" policy problems because each is too limited by its "liberal" worldview. Thus poverty cannot be eliminated by either markets or welfare. But the language and culture of politics precludes more drastic approaches. The limits of political action are set by the culture which politics cannot transcend. American political myths are both resources for and constraints on our policy achievements.

This understanding of American politics and policy may provide a test of the earlier analysis of our political culture. Rather than being transcended, central cultural themes are repeated again and again, albeit in new political forms and in response to new problems. American liberalism is characterized by a tension between democratic and economic individualism that is never fully resolved. Politics thus oscillates between these values according to the necessities of the time. The term "cycles" is sometimes used to depict this reality. However, the idea of a cycle connotes an unvarying determinism that denies freedom and creativity to political leaders. They are simply fated to carry out their prescribed historical roles according to those forces that determine the sequences of cycles. A pure conception of cycles depicts successive phases being repeated in a predictable sequence according to a cause or causes that are internally generated by the cycles themselves. However, if we disregard determinism and focus on patterns of alternation in politics and policy, it becomes possible to analyze historical sequences in which a number of factors are interrelated and vary together.[21] The succession of sequences is driven by the political actions of leaders animated and bounded by culture. And the incompleteness of each regime accounts for the repetitive pattern. It is not possible to predict what will happen in the future, but it may be possible to explain the cluster of variables within each cycle and the reasons why one sequence gives way to the next. The sequences in twentieth-century presidential politics is shown in this table.

Preparation	*Achievement*	*Consolidation*
Theodore Roosevelt	Woodrow Wilson	Warren Harding
William Howard Taft		Calvin Coolidge
		Herbert Hoover
	Franklin Roosevelt	Dwight Eisenhower
	Harry Truman	
John Kennedy	Lyndon Johnson	Richard Nixon
		Gerald Ford
Jimmy Carter	Ronald Reagan	George Bush
Bill Clinton		

The table distinguishes among presidents who prepare the way for reform, those who achieve reform, and those who consolidate the achievements without further innovation. Then, as the presidents of consolidation ignore emerging problems, the sequences begin again. The direction of the sequences was broadly progressive until the turn in a conservative direction with Carter and Reagan; the sequences now may be reversing direction with Clinton. The switch from a progressive to a conservative direction permits conservative presidents of achievement to challenge the policy accomplishments of their liberal predecessors and to seek to undo some of them. But conservative presidents of consolidation then moderate those departures from the past and pave the way for new progressive challenges.

It is necessary to have presidents of both preparation and achievement because of the time needed and the difficulties that must be overcome to construct policy coalitions in American politics. Presidents of preparation do not mobilize sufficient political resources, in the form of election victories and congressional majorities, to be presidents of achievement. Presidents of achievement engage in bursts of reform that cannot be sustained for any length of time. They draw on unusual electoral and congressional majorities that they eventually lose.

Political parties are resources for would-be presidents and presidents. But the succession of administrations is not a description of the alternation of progressive and conservative parties in the White House. Theodore Roosevelt and his lieutenant William Howard Taft divided the Republican party in 1912, which permitted Woodrow Wilson to win and carry out a reform program. Jimmy Carter tried to bring the Democratic coalition back to the ideological and programmatic center and unwittingly paved the way for Ronald Reagan. Even if Michael Dukakis had beaten George Bush in 1988, he would have had to have been a president of consolidation, albeit a progressive one, unlike the conservative Bush. There was little support for progressive reform, and there were strong demands for consolidation and modification of the achievements of the Reagan period. Bill Clinton is now experiencing the frustrations of the Carter administration in leading from the center.

Contingencies may enter the schema and throw it off. There was no president of preparation before Franklin Roosevelt because the Depression began so suddenly and dramatically in 1929. One could depict Hoover's attempts to end the Depression as a harbinger of the New Deal. This would follow from the insight that the sequences follow each other in turn. By the same token, Taft, Truman, and Ford were not creative forces in domestic politics and policy, but continued the work of their immediate predecessors.

This formulation is built on domestic politics and policy alone and is grounded in my understanding of American political culture. Domestic politics drives the sequences and provides legitimacy for the domestic policies and programs that follow. Issues of foreign policy may help decide elections, but they do not influence the succession of administrations. There were relationships between domestic politics and foreign policy during the Cold War period, however, as seen in this table.

Interventionists	*Consolidators*
Harry Truman	Dwight Eisenhower
John Kennedy	Richard Nixon
Lyndon Johnson	Gerald Ford
Ronald Reagan	Jimmy Carter

Bill Clinton (?)

One may contend that Nixon had an active foreign policy that belied the label, but his goal was to stabilize relations with the Soviet Union and China and limit American commitments abroad. The dividing line appears to have been the degree of presidential optimism about the ability to pay for Cold War policies. Interventionist presidents were convinced that the American economy could pay for both guns and butter. The presidents of periods of economic slowdown—Nixon, Ford, and Carter—set limits on American intervention abroad.[22] There also may be a correspondence between interventionist presidents and a belief that the instruments of national power can be used and yet controlled that the more cautious presidents lack.

The end of the Cold War may see new patterns, but it is too soon to say. Recent events have indicated progressive reluctance to commit to action abroad and conservative enthusiasm for intervention.

To return to domestic politics and policy, changes from one sequence to the next are driven by four factors:

1. Social and economic problems develop over long periods of time and are eventually perceived by the politically active as requiring government action.
2. Remedies for the problems are discussed by scholars, advocates, journalists, and politicians. Ideas chase problems, and problems chase ideas.

3. Political opportunities to shift the sequence of politics to a new
   period appear, and presidential candidates and many other politicians exploit these opportunities in election promises.
4. During the periods of achievement, politicians and others in opposition develop corrective remedies to unsuccessful policies and, if
   successful politically, will come to power in periods of consolidation, at which point the sequences begin again.

There is nothing deterministic about the sequences. There is no guarantee that the periods will occur at given intervals of time. Fulfillment
depends on the visibility of problems and the skill of politicians at
exploiting them. The ideas that are advanced as plausible remedies for
emerging problems need not solve or even ameliorate them but to the
degree that they appear to do so the presidents of achievement may
hold onto office longer than would otherwise be the case. The president
is not the sole mover in such political and policy innovation. An electoral sweep is produced by large numbers of the politically active—
including not only politicians, but policy advocates and the media—to
whom voters respond favorably, and the role of presidents in such a
coalition, both in elections and in governing, is indeterminate. It should
be possible to assess the relative importance of presidential leadership
and political skill in presidencies of achievement, and the following
chapters on three presidents are intended to do so.

Party alternations need not occur as they have occurred in the
twentieth century. Thomas Dewey could have won the presidential
election in 1948, just as Nixon could have prevailed in 1960. Ford and
Dukakis might have won, and Clinton might have lost to Bush. Such
close elections may turn on short-term factors that cannot necessarily
be assigned to the cyclic model. Conversely, big electoral changes are
best explained by the theory: Roosevelt, Eisenhower, and perhaps the
Johnson and Reagan reelection victories. The logic of the sequences
provides a historical context for explaining politics and policy without determinism. Had close elections swung the other way, the logic
of the sequence pattern still would have held good. Dewey would
have been a president of consolidation, and Nixon might have been

more of a progressive had he immediately followed Eisenhower. He was pushed somewhat into a conservative mold by succeeding Johnson and the disruptions of Great Society programs. A second Ford term would not have been innovative, and if Carter had defeated Reagan the uncertain direction of his presidency might have been even more acute than in his first term.

This analysis suggests that a president's discernment of the political resources and constraints of the historical moment may make a difference in how well he helps bring about a change in sequence and fulfills the possibilities opened up by his election. Theodore Roosevelt was an extremely skillful president of preparation. He hoped to be a president of achievement, but recognized the limits placed on action by the politics of his time. Kennedy appears to have understood the same thing and prepared his domestic program in anticipation of a major victory in 1964; indeed, Johnson achieved that victory. Both Carter and Clinton overestimated what could be achieved in presidencies of preparation and failed accordingly. Franklin Roosevelt, Eisenhower, Johnson, and Reagan appear to have discerned what was possible in their time and have acted to take advantage of their opportunities. Thus presidents are not simply thrust into historical roles prepared by others. They help to fashion the popular expectations with which they enter the presidency, and they fulfill those expectations with varying degrees of political skill.

This picture of politics refers only to twentieth-century history, in which the central, continuing issue has been the proper role of the federal government in a nation of states and a society with strong concentrations of private economic power. In the first half of the century, the overriding issue was the role of government in regulating business and ensuring the health of the economy. In the second half of the century, the main point of contention has been the role of the central government in providing income and benefits to disadvantaged groups in society, but without a resolution of the earlier questions about the responsibility of government for regulating business and keeping the economy healthy. Presidencies of achievement have depended on continual economic growth, despite recessions and depressions, because without growth the expanding role of government and the costs of activist government cannot be easily justified.

The idea of sequences has much in common with the Schlesingers' interpretations of political eras. The main differences are my inclusion of a period of preparation in my model and my deemphasis of internally driven sequences. But both formulations share the belief that the periods are anchored in the conflicts within American liberalism and that each is a cluster of related variables. However, I do not insist on a progressive interpretation of American history; the sequences may run in either a progressive or a conservative direction.

It is important to distinguish this idea of sequences from the question of party realignment or dealignment, which has deviled both politics and political science since 1968. The election of governments in which the president and the majority of members of Congress belong to different parties has become the norm since Nixon served with a Democratic Congress. As the New Deal coalition eroded in a series of elections beginning in 1952, the Republicans have not been able to fashion a comparable majority coalition that would control both the White House and Congress. Waiting for realignment is like waiting for Godot, in the Samuel Beckett play; he never comes. But the idea of sequences does not depend on realignment or dealignment. A schema of sequences driven by the tensions within American political culture would play out in different ways, depending on partisan fortunes. But as long as the main cultural theme is that of tension between democratic and economic individualism, we will elect presidents of preparation, achievement, and consolidation.

❖ ❖ ❖

PUBLIC OPINION AND HISTORICAL CHANGE

To establish the plausibility of the idea of sequences of politics and policy in modern American history, one must show that popular opinion has both responded to and guided the leadership of politicians in such sequential patterns. One would then have a conception of political leaders working in slowly moving fields of social change and politics.[23]

The conception of "strategic" leadership assumes that intelligent political leaders choose goals commensurate with the available political resources and that the supply of such resources is always limited. American political institutions compound this task because of the many formal and informal barriers to innovation. Therefore, the key to effective leadership in a complex governmental process is the ability to discern emerging dilemmas for which remedies must be found and behind which coalitions can be assembled. This is a markedly decentralized and lengthy procedure. Presidents work at the top of the process, and thus wait for important issues to become salient to a great many actors. Their job is the final orchestration of agreement. Presidential entrepreneurship is duplicated by the policy entrepreneurship of countless others.

In each period of preparation, there are policy entrepreneurs in Congress, advocacy groups, research institutions, foundations, and many other kinds of organizations, working to find answers to problems that the incumbent president is not addressing. Much of this work is hidden from the general public, and it becomes visible only when political entrepreneurs publicly offer remedies for unresolved problems. In the 1950s, members of Congress developed many of the reform ideas about full employment, health insurance, management of the economy, and federal aid to education that were later co-opted by Kennedy and Johnson as their programs. By the same token, the ideas of supply-side economics and of a smaller role for the federal government in social programs that the Reagan administration carried into office had been developed during the previous years of opposition by Republican members of Congress and researchers at conservative think tanks like the Heritage Foundation.

Ideas in good currency are not direct expressions of public opinion or public demands. At this point in the process, the public—or, rather, the many publics—is responsive to the articulation of new problems. Surveys reveal public concern about dirty air, rising fear of crime, or uneasiness about affirmative action. A senator is reelected in a special election after hitting hard on the issues of health care for the elderly and the working poor. Politicians look for these kinds of signs as a prerequisite for getting a fresh issue on the public agenda. The task of politicians is then to seek political support for the issues that they are championing. They create the public clamor in cooperation with all kinds of policy advocates.[24] The proposed solutions are then organized by politicians in competing sets of ideas. Presidents and their lieutenants play the most visible role in this process, but they harness such processes rather than dominate them.

Politicians seldom change people's minds with their rhetoric. They do not seek converts. The shifts in the sequences of politics do not occur because many voters suddenly change their minds about a question on which they have had strong opinions. Rather, sequences change when politicians are able to forge winning coalitions behind new issues about which public opinion is still fluid. Political rhetoric can move popular opinion in such cases. Publics and other politicians respond to fresh ideas about how to resolve a given problem because they are not committed to any one solution. Such issues are the entering wedge for shifts in the political mood of the country and the sequences of governance.[25]

Politicians can be said to follow public opinion when they defer to clear and strongly held beliefs and attitudes at the median point of public opinion. This is true whether opinion is consensual or divided. The demand for clean air and the deep conflict over abortion illustrate how opinions at the median point may either empower or paralyze politicians. But in either case, political leaders are following rather than leading. Democratic leadership occurs when politicians succeed in moving the median point in the distribution of public opinion toward the positions that they take publicly. This is most likely to succeed with new issues about which there is popular concern but no agreement on remedies. John Geer makes a nice distinction between leadership in which political rhetoric persuades a large audience to change their minds and leadership in which the words of politicians move key parts of the public from uncertainty to a firm position. Abraham Lincoln both followed and led opinion in regard to the Emancipation Proclamation. He knew the limits beyond which he could not go in calling for the abolition of slavery—for example, in the border states. But he also cleverly used tangible facts, such as the need for more manpower for military victory, to rally opinion behind the emancipation of slaves in the Confederacy. In contrast, George Bush provided no leadership in regard to highly salient issues like health care, and his uncertainty bred uncertainty. He chose not to lead when he might have done so. To lead would have required presenting plausible proposals that could win enough political support among enough people to shift the median opinion in the president's direction.

A good politician and a creative leader are not the same. But creative democratic leaders must also be skillful politicians. They add a talent for exploiting emerging issues that conventional politicians avoid. Creative leaders must also be followers; otherwise, they would not recognize the potential exploitability of given issues. Politicians engage in political education when they seek to lead on new issues.

American politics and government often appear to be in equilibrium or even in a state of "stasis" of political and policy deadlock. But to say this is to ignore the continual press for change that surfaces in periods of policy innovation. The driving force is issue development, in which positive feedback from followers to the initiatives of leaders builds on itself and allows for innovation.[26] Political rhetoric is especially important to issue development because it presents "policy images" that are combinations of what can be done and what should be done. Competing politicians tell diverse causal stories about welfare, health care, or national defense that are appeals to cultural beliefs in a new guise. The politicians who win have done so with their stories and symbols. Skillful political leaders can "force an onrushing of the tide" and use their talents to push the current in a given direction.

❖ ❖ ❖

POLICY MOODS, COLLECTIVE OPINION, AND LEADERSHIP

A discussion of the relation of public opinion to popular politics and, ultimately, to what governments, led by politicians, do must make two assumptions: public opinion has collective properties that cannot be tapped simply by aggregating the views of many individuals, and it changes over time in response to events and the rhetoric of politicians. Collective opinion can be shown to be "rational" in that it can be explained by the changing historical context of social, economic, and political life. Public opinion about political issues does not display radical shifts, but it changes at the margins and may be stimulated by politicians but also will give politicians the leeway to act in new directions. It is a mistake to regard democratic citizens only as individuals. They are anchored in a "social environment" that generates patterns of collective opinion in response to that environment. Individual opinion may be unstable, but public opinion in the aggregate reveals "predictability and stability." It is possible to see changes in public moods over time that produce a moving middle in which electorates are signaling that they will support or resist given policy innovations. Quite often, such opinion shifts are apparent across a number of loosely linked issues, indicating parallel public moods or predispositions. The ideas may be quite general—for example, a concern that government is too big or is inattentive to certain problems. New ideas or policy images may spread very rapidly across issue domains. Thus it may be misleading to assume that support for increased spending for education or welfare is driven by opinion within each policy domain; instead, it may reflect concerns about the state of the nation that undergird specific positions on issues. Such underlying mood changes may be stronger than the particular issue stands themselves. For example, James Stimson found that support for progressive political ideas developed in the late 1950s and peaked in the mid-1960s followed by a turn in a conservative direction in the late 1960s; conservative attitudes diminished somewhat in the late 1970s, but then reached new heights in the 1980s, with a subsequent move in a progressive direction in the late 1980s. Politicians try to be responsive to such underlying moods in the public, insofar as they discern them.[27] For example, as a candidate for president in 1988, George Bush explicitly played to the achievements of the Reagan presidency, but also signaled that he would be more moderate in his desire for "a kinder, gentler nation." And Bush's failure to discern popular unhappiness with a faltering economy in 1992 cost him reelection. By the same token, Clinton was more attuned than Bush to changing policy moods in 1992, but may have lost touch very quickly if the 1994 congressional elections were a harbinger of dissatisfaction with his presidency.

Does this mean that there are policy mandates that politicians may invoke as support for their policies once they are in office? This is not literally the case. Many voters are uncertain or even ignorant about issues. They vote to punish incumbents as much as or more than they vote to ratify or reject a proposed program. Yet winning politicians invariably claim a mandate. And especially dramatic elections are turning points in public policy that seem to have been responsive to public desire for change. How else explain the public-policy consequences of the 1932, 1964, and 1980 presidential elections? There is a mandate in the sense of a discernible voter shift in public mood. A winning president and a large majority of the president's party in Congress reflect this swing. The analysis of voters as individuals, and even groups, may not provide evidence of such mandates. But a look at underlying moods of public opinion across time may reveal such patterns. There is often a "moderate" central tendency in such shifts in which large parts of the public are saying "do more" or "do less."

Such shifts reflect the concern of voters for the nation's general welfare that is not the sum of group demands. Even when there are clear differences of opinion among social and economic groups, opinion within each group moves in the same general direction, hinting at the presence of "parallel publics."[28]

Stimson has posited "cycles" of politics and policy in which a moving middle of mainstream opinion gives permission for governments to act in accordance with the public mood. The reversal of such an affirmation may eventually occur, but the sequences will vary in strength and length of time and may not return to where they started. The metaphor of tidal waves is better than that of a pendulum. The tide goes out and comes in, but the waves may be very different in successive tides. It is to be expected that every policy regime will eventually undermine itself by failure to adapt to new conditions, and the cycle will then turn again.

The principal influences on the collective policy ideas of Americans are social and economic trends and national and world events. Perceptions are filtered through interpreters, whether politicians, the media, or local opinion leaders. Scholars who study public opinion agree that ordinary people are quite capable of assessing trends and events according to their own experiences in everyday life if political leaders do not attempt to distort facts and mislead citizens in their interpretations. Ben Page defined "good" public opinion as "true, authentic or enlightened interests in terms of fully informed preferences." Those who try to give publics "good" information educate, and those who seek to manipulate through untruths and distortions mislead the public. Of course, it is difficult to distinguish education and manipulation, but ordinary people can arrive at reasonable conclusions about their political choices if their information is adequate to the task. The absence of basic information about issues should not be equated with the failure of voters to understand their choices in elections. Voters should be regarded not as scholars who assess alternatives and weigh evidence, but as clinicians who make inferential leaps between their own situations and what they hear from politicians. They decide if the stories of leaders make sense in terms of their own lives. Much of the information of daily life is thus homework for voting decisions. By the same token, it is difficult for political leaders to identify and discuss issues whose connections to the everyday lives of voters seem tenuous. Citizens will not be persuaded by academic theories about the dangers of a budget deficit, for example, that they do not feel in their own lives. They must first experience the consequences of a social or an economic problem, and then will respond to alternative solutions proposed by political leaders.[29]

These processes of "collective deliberation," as they are presently understood, call on public opinion to be more than the sum of its parts. One thinks of James Madison's words in *The Federalist*, No. 63, about the "cool and deliberate sense of the community," which, he felt, ought to prevail in government. John Dewey thought about the public in the same terms, as an "organized, articulate public." Such processes require "trustworthy cue givers" for their efficient operation. Citizens need not master all issues, but may draw informally on many sources of information as they feel their way to their political choices.[30]

❖ ❖ ❖

CONTINUITY AND DISCONTINUITY OF VALUES AND BELIEFS

A fundamental political value like belief in freedom and equality is rooted in the culture and persists over time. It is not the product of political life. But important policy debates are most often about conflicts among values. Changing social circumstances can elevate some values over others and change the character of the trade-offs among values. Ordinary people will use their understanding of these values not in abstract ideological terms, but as aids to deciding how to register their political support. Such thinking is not dichotomous, but is on a continuum in which competing values are balanced according to felt necessities.[31] For example, there are two overlapping majorities among American voters. One majority appears to favor the Democrats on economic issues, while the other is more conservative on social and cultural issues. Thus swing voters may turn to the Democrats if they are worried about the economy, but will not vote for more liberal Democrats because of their views on social issues. These voters prefer the social conservatism of Republicans, but are in no sense economic conservatives. The direction and amount of swing over time, in which partisanship and ideology are in tension, depends on the issues that swing voters are most worried about.[32]

Americans as a people have absorbed the political culture and see its "fault lines," but do not resolve the tensions in ways that make them consistently progressive or conservative. For example, supporters of the welfare state also believe in the values of self-help. The redistribution of income may be regarded as both a limitation on freedom and a path toward individual freedom. When ordinary citizens evoke such values, they are not parroting the more ideological beliefs of active political partisans, but adjusting their diffuse sense of values in tension according to the moment. American political culture provides few egalitarian arguments that would support the kind of thorough-going welfare state common in Western Europe. Dislike of big government has real meaning for people, but this does not mean that most people are ideological conservatives. The support for welfare measures for the less fortunate must be based on humanitarian, not egalitarian, grounds. But support for specific welfare programs may be very high at a given time because a large number of people in the middle class believe them to be right.[33] Swings in the national political mood are to be expected, given the tensions within American liberalism about the role of government. Politics and policy in a democratic polity will shift back and forth between the two kinds of individualism, depending on economic and social conditions.[34] Scholars analyze such changes according to the ideology with which they interpret American history and politics, but ordinary people see no need for such theories. They embody the reality.

American politics and policy are anchored in the fruitful tension within the broad ideology of liberalism as Louis Hartz defines it. Conservative individualism, in democratic form, promises material abundance for all. Progressive reform is justified and accepted only if it claims to create greater opportunities for individuals to make their way in life. We thus see the paradox that politicians can rally publics to stand behind "collective goods" in matters of liberty and equality only if such public goods are to enhance the opportunities of individuals. Our collectivism, in uniquely American form, is anchored in individualism.

This exposition of American political culture sets the stage for the analysis of presidents that follows. The prophets of the Bible were authentic figures to the community to which they preached because they appealed to the shared values of the faithful. Presidents, at their best, do the same. The preaching must be tempered by prudence. It does not always succeed, and it may not even be appropriate for the normal transactional politics of the day. But teaching and preaching are vital to the constructive resolution of issues relevant to the essential purposes of the Union.

4

Franklin D. Roosevelt

❖ ❖ ❖ ❖ ❖ ❖ ❖ ❖ ❖ ❖ ❖ ❖ ❖ ❖

Franklin Roosevelt was a supremely skilled politician and is the exemplar of the good leader of the polity in this book. His highly proficient skills of persuasion were the most important thing about his leadership. He knew how to lead by listening and teaching, and then listening and learning more, as he again taught. He could sense what was in people's minds at any given historical moment and articulate plausible remedies for their concerns.

He was a child of privilege in an old Hudson Valley aristocracy, a background that gave him great self-confidence at the same time that it kept him apart from the money changers of his day, the new business classes. The only child of a doting young mother and an older father, he grew up to expect to be the center of attention; yet, to maintain his privacy in the face of such a smothering love, he kept his thoughts and feelings to himself. At Groton and Harvard, he devoted himself to popularity rather than scholarship. He was editor of the *Harvard Crimson* and marshal of his graduating class. One biographer describes him at that time: "The pleasure gained from the sport of maneuvering and manipulation, and the status that came with political prize, held strongest appeal for him. Unwittingly, in these pursuits he took the first stride toward becoming an effective politician."[1] His co-editor remembered that "in his geniality was a kind of frictionless command."[2]

The practice of law in New York City was far too limiting a world for Roosevelt. He once announced to his fellow law clerks that he intended to pick good Democratic years and be, successively, a member of the New York legislature, Secretary of the Navy, governor of New York, and, with luck, president of the United States. Of course, his distant relative Theodore Roosevelt had followed much the same route, so the path was clear. At the age of thirty-one, in 1913, he became Assistant Secretary of the Navy in Woodrow Wilson's administration, thus placing himself within the sphere of the other great president of the progressive period. In Washington, he developed his knack at getting along with all sorts of people: naval officers, labor leaders, congressmen. Secretary of War Newton D. Baker noticed how FDR educated himself in the arts of conciliation: "Young Roosevelt is very promising, but I should think that he'd wear himself out in the promiscuous and extended contacts he maintains with people. But as I have observed him, he seems to clarify his ideas and teach himself as he goes along by that very conversational method."[3]

Before he was forty, Roosevelt had served in the New York legislature, gained experience in the executive branch in Washington for seven years, and been the Democratic candidate for vice president in 1920. He was a rising star. There is general agreement that the sudden onset of polio, which crippled him for life, did not so much alter Roosevelt's personality as reinforce his congenital optimism, determination, and ambition. He would not admit the possibility of failure, and although he was terribly depressed at times, he radiated courage and cheer to those around him. All those who worked with him then and in later years noticed a certain serenity with which he faced daily challenges. When asked once if things worried him, he replied, "If you had spent two years in bed trying to wiggle your big toes, after that anything else would seem easy."[4]

Harry Hopkins, who was perhaps Roosevelt's closest aide during World War II, once remarked to Robert Sherwood, a playwright who was writing speeches for the president, that FDR had a quality that eluded Hopkins, but he wondered if it was not trust in God: "It seems unreasonable at times, but he falls back on something that gives him complete assurance that everything is going to be alright. Why should he be so sure that it will be alright?"[5]

In February 1933, a man shot at Roosevelt, who was riding in an open car in Miami, but succeeded in killing Anton Cermak, the mayor of Chicago, who was with the president-elect. FDR was calm and decisive, ordering the driver to go immediately to the hospital, paying no attention to his own security, and talking to the wounded man. His calm courage impressed all who saw him.[6]

Roosevelt was very intelligent, but was not widely read and did not place much stock in logic or abstract ideas. He thought with his whole personality. Frances Perkins put it this way: "His emotions, his intuitive understanding, his imagination, his moral and traditional bias, his sense of right and wrong—all entered into his mind and unless these flowed freely through his mind as he considered a subject, he was unlikely to come to any clear conclusion or ever to a clear understanding."[7]

Those who worked with him closely saw that he had an intellect of great range and subtlety. His mind was like a gyroscope. One consequence was that he took his time making difficult decisions, telling no one of the cross-currents in his thinking; what seemed like procrastination may have been the deliberate artifice of patience and the hope that a pattern would eventually emerge. His cognitive style and his optimism were in harmony. He once told a reporter who asked him about his philosophy that he was "a Christian and a Democratic—that's all." He had blended a sense of duty and service anchored in his secure social identity with a progressivism that he had learned from his cousin Theodore and from Woodrow Wilson.

Roosevelt's political personality was a unity. He drew strength for leadership from empathy and connections established with others, both individuals and large audiences. He used his charm to dominate and, at the same time, to inspire and encourage others to act in his service. He was flexible in his thinking and maneuvering, perhaps to a fault, for he resisted all theories as a basis for action. He knew how to weave a web of action, from competing advisers, in public appeals, and in feeling his way toward politically viable legislation. He loved politics of all kinds, with himself at the center. These virtues had corresponding faults, and he would not have been such a talented political man had he not had a shadow side. The great physical and psychological demands on the kind of president he sought to be require a deep personal need to lead. At the core of the shadow was a demand to win the attention and affection of others. He was always acting, even in the smallest details of his personal life, and always conscious that he was on stage. His close personal assistant Sam Rosenman remembered that side of Roosevelt when campaigning with the president:

> Thoroughly experienced public speaker though he was, he was generally very nervous as the time to get up to deliver his speech drew near. He seldom found any pleasure at a meeting or at a banquet until his speech had actually begun. He nervously smoked cigarette after cigarette. His hand would shake as he drank water. While waiting to be introduced he would fidget in his chair. Once he had gotten to his feet and said, "My friends," he was a changed man—relaxed, in perfect touch with his audience, every fibre concentrated on what he was saying and in the effect it was producing—all traces of nervousness gone.[8]

This was the nervousness of the talented actor and performer, and it is a necessary ingredient of good performance in artists of all kinds. It is not necessarily a neurotic fear or insecurity. The need to win over others and capture attention could inflate Roosevelt's sense of expansive confidence that he could prevail in all situations. The very buoyancy and optimism that were the bases of his persuasive skills, and his belief that everything would be all right in time, could also cause him to overreach out of miscalculated self-confidence. If he ever stopped listening or learning and failed to test political reality, he could substitute undue self-confidence for skill and thereby fail.

The Greek god Mercury was the "messenger" who carried good news to all parts of the world. This was FDR's greatest skill. But in Greek legend, Mercury was also the "trickster," a playful manipulator of others. The trickster side of Roosevelt was best seen in his manipulative stratagems, but they often undercut his effectiveness. At his best, the trickster was subdued by his sense of prudence. At his very best, he combined moral purpose and prudence. His emotional security made him free to discern what was politically possible and therefore temper his confidence with a sense of limits. Once he was so anchored, his rhetorical abilities gave him the capacity to "teach reality."

Paul Appleby's description of Roosevelt sums up the complex political man:

> His use of that skill [of managing people] was deeply habitual. It was the kind of opportunism intrinsically related to democratic leadership. He was, in a high level sense, a planner, always looking forward, calculating the future in terms of a variety of alternatives, always developing out of a set of current alternatives. It was this quality that enabled him to encourage different men along somewhat different or competitive lines. . . . He was a pluralistic leader of a pluralistic people.[9]

❖ ❖ ❖

ROOSEVELT'S LIBERALISM

Roosevelt campaigned for the New York governorship in 1928, and again in 1930, as a "progressive." He offered themes of reform, in contrast to the Republican litany of prosperity of the 1920s. But he also defended himself against any possible charge of being a "radical." He was to take this middle course for the rest of his career. He saw himself as a new kind of Democratic leader, symbolized by his unprecedented airplane flight to Chicago to accept the nomination of the Democratic National Convention in person. He meant to take charge of his party, dominated by big-city machine politicians and southern conservatives, as he worked with its members in practical politics. The convention gave him the party, and he never gave it back. A new Democratic coalition of farmers, labor, minorities, and most of the Republican and Democratic "progressives" was to emerge and dominate American presidential politics until 1968.

It is the conventional wisdom that Roosevelt played it safe in the 1932 campaign and advocated no departures in policy beyond promising to bring the country out of its economic ills. In fact, most of the themes of New Deal programs were expressed in his campaign speeches, although in guarded fashion as tentative proposals. The more important question is whether Roosevelt entered office with a coherent philosophy, and the answer is clearly yes. He is often depicted as an opportunistic pragmatist who launched one New Deal experiment after another without concern for the larger picture. In truth, he took the ideas and leadership style of Thomas Jefferson as his guide and adapted both to the political and policy issues he faced. He was thus able to anchor the New Deal within the dominant themes of American political culture. The presidency is not an agency for the articulation of political philosophy; yet we have seen Lincoln redefine the American constitutional tradition, and in 1932 and the years after, FDR and Herbert Hoover argued publicly over who was the real heir of Jefferson's politics and principles. Such debate is necessary because presidents must anchor their specific programs in larger appeals to the spirit of the Constitution. In this regard, they draw on a history of rhetorical discourse as old as the republic itself. Placing his presidency in this stream of discourse is a way for a president to achieve what Philip Abbott calls "self-understanding."[10]

In the Jefferson example, the enemy is Alexander Hamilton, who favored placing the authority of government behind the worlds of business and manufacture. Jefferson resisted such policies because he feared that the yeoman farmer, who was the backbone of his ideal democracy, would be exploited by a strong central government in league with commerce. This caused Jeffersonians, and Jacksonians after them, to favor limited government. Roosevelt argued that Hoover and other modern individualists did not understand that the modern corporate world had become a threat to the individualism of ordinary citizens because of its control over their lives and fortunes. For Hoover, any move toward increasing the power of the federal government, in order to place checks on business, was virtually "un-American." Hoover saw the Great Depression in the United States as originating in problems of the world economy. Therefore, few things could be done in domestic policy to bring recovery. Roosevelt disagreed strongly and put the blame for the Depression on the excesses of American capitalism. He reinterpreted Jefferson to call for the use of national government and presidential power to restore individualism to Americans by checking the private power of business. Hoover and Roosevelt were competitors in the interpretation of the purposes of government.

Roosevelt's effort to create a philosophical basis for the New Deal is evident in his campaign speech to the Commonwealth Club of San Francisco. The speech was intended as a refutation of Hoover's interpretation of American individualism. Roosevelt's alternative was the thesis that the national government must redress the inequalities and lost opportunities created by business. The author of the first draft of the Commonwealth Club speech was Columbia University law professor Adolf Berle, Jr., one of FDR's original "brain trusters." Berle's draft had the candidate declare that the liberalism of Wilson, in its desire to break up corporate power by trust-busting and return the country to an earlier individualism, was no longer appropriate. Rather, Berle hoped to be the voice of a radicalism that would advocate planning and national control of economic life. Robert Eden's close analysis of the writing of the speech shows that FDR taught Berle more than Berle ever knew about reviving old ideas for new purposes.[11]

Eden depicts Berle's thinking as much like that of the philosopher John Dewey, who in the early 1930s was calling for an entirely new intellectual effort to replace the old liberalism of individualism with a new liberalism more in keeping with communitarian values. Dewey hoped that in time such an intellectual movement would become the basis for a third political party. He saw no hope in either of the major political parties and voted for Norman Thomas, the Socialist candidate for president, in 1932. But Dewey did not understand that creative politicians may be more innovative than intellectuals because they have to invent new ideas and adapt old ones while doing their work. This was certainly the case with FDR, who showed Berle how to adapt Jefferson's ideas, so legitimate in American political culture, to new challenges. Roosevelt brought Jefferson up to date by arguing that the third president had based his support for limited government on his fear of giant combinations of governmental and economic power in Hamiltonian policies. A pragmatic liberal in 1932 would adapt the Jeffersonian credo to an understanding that combinations of private corporate power threatened the individualism that Jefferson had valued. It was Hoover who held to the outdated formal liberalism of governmental forms in their original conception.

The task of leadership according to FDR was to "redefine the rights of the governed" in modern conditions. Theodore Roosevelt and Woodrow Wilson had been moving in the same direction, not only in formulating policies, but in seeing the presidency as an agency of such efforts. The presidency was to be an office of administrative power fully responsive to public opinion. Dewey's more abstract thought could not envision such executive power as the instrument of ideas. He had no interest in political biography. Roosevelt took John Locke's ideas, which had been preached by American conservatives in a pallid fervor for limited government, and gave them a strength found in Britain and other European nations and explicit in Locke's appeal to strong executive action in crisis. Formal liberalism, as invoked by Hoover, could not adapt to new economic conditions, and the pragmatic liberalism of the New Deal thus became extraordinarily resilient in practice, but with a general philosophical underpinning. Democratic government could be regarded as experimental in regard to particular programs once it was accepted that government had the right and responsibility to experiment.

Roosevelt created the political language with which American politics has been conducted from his time to our own. In this pragmatic liberalism, the role of government acting on behalf of the public welfare, however conceived, is a matter of more or less action. The president, for FDR, was the voice of the people and the principal constitutional officer rather than one among three. FDR created the conditions for the idealization of presidential power.

This conception of the presidency can be interpreted in both Aristotelian and Machiavellian terms. The president is to "teach the spirit of the constitution." He is to teach reality. But the way is open for the president to use artifice and to seek his own power and glory. The line between constitutional authority and personal aggrandizement is not so clear. Roosevelt, the tribune of the people, was certainly a democrat. But Roosevelt the politician was a thoroughly political man. We are back with Henry V. Niccolò Machiavelli invented the modern idea of the executive leader, and the American presidency carries that legacy with it even today. Of course, FDR was not a demagogue or an abuser of power; as we will see, he used artifice and misleading demagogy at times. But the important point is that with the idealization of presidential leadership as the key to the public good, we become very dependent on the person who is president. A politically weak president may assert the power of the presidential office, but abuse the presidential powers. Roosevelt's presidency dramatized these competing possibilities.

VICTORY AND THE HUNDRED DAYS

Roosevelt won 54 percent of the popular vote in the 1932 election. The Democratic majorities in the House and Senate were large. Democrats had not controlled both houses of Congress since 1916. And in the midterm election of 1934, in which presidential majorities in Congress usually dwindle, the Democrats gained even more seats. However, it must not be forgotten that 167 of Roosevelt's 472 electoral votes came from 16 southern and border states, in which the Democrats were firmly established by political history but were not as progressive in their acceptance of government as the New Deal credo required.[12] The new president had a mandate to act boldly, but, from the beginning, there were strong constraints on and misgivings about his exercise of power.

Roosevelt's inaugural address, with its stirring words that the only thing to fear was fear itself, gave hope that someone was finally in charge. His closing words make this clear: "The people of the United States have not failed. In their need they have registered a mandate that they want direct, vigorous action. They have asked for discipline and direction under leadership. They have made me the direct instrument of their wishes. In the spirit of the gift, I take it."[13] The confidence of the electorate and of Congress had been shattered, and the popular demand for action permitted the new president to fill the vacuum temporarily.

From March 9 to June 16, 1933, the so-called Hundred Days, Roosevelt urged and Congress passed laws stabilizing and regulating banking, shoring up farm and home mortgages, creating unemployment-relief agencies, regulating securities, and setting up broad plans to reduce agricultural production to avoid wasteful surpluses and to encourage cooperative planning among business, labor, and government in order to stimulate purchasing power in the economy.[14] Three main purposes were intertwined: unemployment relief, economic recovery, and reform of institutions to prevent future depressions. Roosevelt told his aides that he must strike while the Congress was hot, and a stream of ideas flowed from the White House to Capitol Hill.

But Roosevelt was no dictator. Even in all the euphoria, there were constraints. The first was his own caution. He had always been a Jeffersonian and a Wilsonian, and thus he rejected any radical possibilities, such as nationalizing the banking system, as some of his advisers urged. He was responsive to the many contradictory pressure groups whose support was necessary for legislative action, and he spoke in terms of consensus rather than conflict. He also relied very heavily on the experienced senior congressional leaders, both Democratic and Republican, many of whom had been fighting for the progressive cause for years. He used his press conferences and his radio talks to the general public to explain his goals and pull Congress into that discourse. And he quite often gave way when Congress indicated its displeasure with a particular matter. He used all the persuasive powers at his command, spending hours on the telephone and in private meetings with members of Congress. Thus even with the overwhelming support for bold action, the new president was not a dictator but a tribune and an orchestrator. He made himself, and his magnetic public personality, the symbol of action, and he justified action by persuasive rhetoric. But even the strongest popular support did not enable him to forgo bargaining and compromise as the Hundred Days took legislative form. His tactical skills were indispensable, but they were the instruments of his larger strategic appeals and purposes.

The theme of what came to be called the first New Deal was cooperation for recovery on a large scale. Farmers were to plant fewer crops and thus increase agricultural prices for their own recuperation. Business and labor, steered by the National Recovery Administration (NRA), were to slowly revive economic confidence and put people back to work. This model of recovery was loosely based on the economy of World War I, in which the Wilson administration coordinated all sectors of the economy in the war effort. Relief jobs for the unemployed were intended to be temporary until the economy revived.

The great difficulty was that there was no body of economic theory that might have guided the New Deal toward economic recovery. Orthodox economics would cut government spending and wait for business confidence to revive. FDR knew that this doctrine was bankrupt, both politically and economically, and therefore the New Deal was a series of experiments from which new theories might emerge. He had no understanding of the idea of deliberate deficit spending by government to put new purchasing power in the hands of citizens so that the economy might be revived. The theories of the British economist John Maynard Keynes, which were to become the new economic orthodoxy after World War II, were not available to or understood by enough people.[15]

For these reasons, as well as his own style of learning when listening to point–counterpoint discussions, Roosevelt was quite happy to let his advisers fight through contradictory courses of action in meetings with him and to encourage them all. He listened both to advocates of national planning and to their critics, who wanted more competition in the economy. His vision of America embraced many competing principles, in which coordination and competition, national power and administrative decentralization, nationalism and internationalism all were important. He saw himself as the juggler who would balance them all. Others were never sure where he was going in given cases, and perhaps he wondered as well.[16]

❖ ❖ ❖

THE SECOND NEW DEAL

The great political lift that Roosevelt had given the nation in his first years was, however, not accompanied by a corresponding economic lift. More than 10 million people were still unemployed after two years. Demagogic leaders were creating grassroots movements in a "thunder on the left" that challenged the New Deal directly. Senator Huey Long of Louisiana preached a "Share Our Wealth" rhetoric. The Townsend Plan movement called for immediate government pensions for the elderly, and the radio priest Father Charles Coughlin criticized capitalism, bankers, and the timidity of the New Deal. There was also "thunder on the right" as conservative opponents of the New Deal railed against its use of national power in the economy. Herbert Hoover, conservative Democrats, and many leaders of big business formed coalitions against the president.

To some observers, the president in early 1935 seemed to have lost his sense of direction as he was buffeted from left and right. But what followed was a burst of political creativity that only Roosevelt could have provided and that led eventually to what historians call the second New Deal. Roosevelt began 1935 by asking Congress to enact a comprehensive Social Security program and increase public-works programs. But he held back on tax reform and labor legislation because he did not want to offend the business community, whose cooperation in economic recovery was so important. But, after the Supreme Court declared the National Recovery Act unconstitutional in May, the president introduced tax reform for greater progressiveness, proposed the breaking up of utility holding companies, and embraced labor legislation to require companies to bargain with unions. These ideas were enacted and, along with Social Security, came to be known as the second New Deal. Roosevelt used these legislative initiatives to reassert his leadership over the Democratic party and steal the thunder of his critics on the left. This, of course, necessarily sharpened his conflicts with his critics on the right.[17]

The second New Deal moved away from the ideal of national planning and toward the Wilsonian principle of increased competition among businesses, with a safety net for those at the bottom of the economic ladder. The Jeffersonian ideal was reaffirmed and given a Jacksonian cast. Yet as the president presented a sharper rhetorical front to the public, he was cautious in what he asked Congress to do and how it was to be done. He accepted the advice of experts for a modest Social Security system focused on pensions for the elderly and stipends for the disabled and widowed. He insisted that Social Security be based on the contributory principle of workers saving for themselves, even though this was not fully accurate, in order to stress self-reliance and to prevent future governments from eliminating benefits.[18] He gave Congress great slack and invoked little public pressure as the legislators addressed the proposals of the second New Deal. He did not wish to be regarded as a dictator and relied on the New Deal Democrats in Congress to bring the conservative Democrats along. He was in no hurry because he would exploit the program ideas politically in the 1936 election. He did not want the voters kept at a fever pitch for long. He skillfully used presidential patronage, public works, and personal cultivation to bring along conservative Democrats in Congress. Even though his reform agenda was clearly progressive, he paid court to conservatives as much as possible. He knew that the opposition of conservative southern Democrats in Congress could defeat his program. He told his aides that he wanted his bills to originate with Congress and relied heavily on key congressional leaders to manage the legislative process and get them passed. It became apparent in 1935 that by pushing southern Democrats to support progressive tax policies and by breaking up utility holding companies, the president had angered a number of conservative Democrats. They began to join the Republicans in opposition, thus forming the core of the "conservative coalition" of 1937 to 1964.

At the same time that Roosevelt had to cultivate congressional conservatives, he had to find ways to direct the restlessness among poor farmers and unemployed and underemployed workers and to get them behind him. He was afraid that Huey Long might run well enough as an independent in a presidential election to deny him reelection in favor of a Republican. The second New Deal was his answer. The assassination of Long in September 1935 eased some of his concerns, and he was quick to reinstate federal patronage denied to Louisiana while Long was alive. He also used work-relief and public-works staff positions in the states to reward political supporters and punish opponents. By the same token, he built strong support in the Democratic machines of the cities, which were also cemented with federal benefits. He was very well informed about politics in all the states and could assess who he could rely on to help him be reelected. At the same time, he focused on economizing in government in response to Republican critics, and cut relief and public-works budgets accordingly. He even declared that the regular 1937 fiscal-year budget was balanced. Public-opinion polls in 1936 showed him to be ahead in the race for president, and as the Republicans denounced him as the "destroyer of the American dream," he placed himself in the middle of the road as the spokesman for traditional American values.

He had, though, succeeded in moving the New Deal beyond the progressive ideology of freedom and competition and had added the element of economic security. The outlines of the new Democratic coalition of urban ethnic groups, farmers, unionized workers, African-Americans, and women began to be clear. Democratic intellectuals provided interpretations of history and politics to characterize the New Deal as a reform movement, and their role in the coalition was very valuable. They could articulate the ideals of a political party as programmatic, which was something of a mystery to most American organizational politicians at that time. The president's discernment of the historical opportunities to build a new majority was more acute than that of his political advisers. He saw politics and policy as complementary resources in ways that most of them did not.

to his teaching. He alone decided when the time was ripe. If he wished to move in a new direction, he pressed a theme gently and then assessed public reaction as it came back to him through many channels. If the reports were encouraging, he moved ahead with caution step by step.

A classic example of Roosevelt's strategy was his treatment of Social Security. He chose not to push for legislation in 1933 because of the concern that the public was not ready. Government support for the old and the weak seemed too alien to the American tradition of self-reliance. He first mentioned the subject in 1934 at a press conference with business editors. He stressed the actuarial soundness of the idea, the importance of workers' financial contributions to old-age pensions, and the limited role of the federal government in such a plan. These words were clearly tailored for his audience. From June 1934 to January 1935, when Social Security legislation was sent to Congress, he pursued an educational campaign that included two fireside chats in which he took great pains to deny that Social Security was a "socialist" idea. He appointed a commission on Social Security to study and recommend proposals to him. He went on tour and presented the idea in several speeches. In January 1935, he discussed it in the State of the Union Message. But after the measure had gone to Capitol Hill, he mentioned it publicly only once before it passed in August. That was in an April fireside chat in which he nudged Congress along. He mentioned the issue often in his press conferences but only on "background," so he could not be quoted or appear to be pressuring Congress. But he kept the issue alive. His strategy all along had been to convince Americans that Social Security was congenial to traditional American values of self-help.[22]

It is very clear that FDR took care to deny the charge of "socialism." He explained Social Security as a logical extension of the constitutional principle of government acting for the general welfare. This was not to be a rejection of American values, but a return to those values that had been ignored during the age of economic growth and expansion. There was no threat to individual freedom in any way. Clearly, he recognized the need to overcome the cultural obstacle of individualism not by preaching a new principle, but by affirming that very individualism in a new form.

There is only limited direct evidence that Roosevelt's rhetorical strategy influenced the passage of the Social Security Act. Secretary of Labor Frances Perkins observed that the public educational effort, not only by the president but by many of his lieutenants, such as herself, appeared to have won wide backing for Social Security among Americans, who urged their members of Congress to support it.[23] The earliest polls on the subject date from December 1935, and the subsequent polls show a continual growth of public support for Social Security in the next few years, often reaching up to 90 percent or better. An analysis of newspaper coverage of Social Security in 1935 also shows that the issue was given considerable coverage on the front pages.[24]

New Deal scholars believe that the Social Security Act was crucial to the forging of the New Deal political coalition in the country. James MacGregor Burns considered all the New Deal programs on the eve of the 1936 presidential election in terms of the great number and variety of groups being helped and concluded that Social Security was the most important for the construction of the new coalition.[25] Rex Tugwell saw Roosevelt's style as the key to acceptance of the new policy:

> When Franklin began to think about this conception, it took hold of his imagination and he proliferated ideas so rapidly— and for once so openly—that none of those about him could keep up with him. Washington for weeks was devoted to speculation about the various possibilities after the infection began to spread out to wider and wider circles. Franklin did nothing to check it. . . . It was not long, however, until social security had a hold on people's minds that demanded attention.

Tugwell added that the enactment of Social Security cemented longtime progressives to the New Deal and brought organized labor into the New Deal camp because the rank and file were so directly affected by the program in their own lives.[26]

Roosevelt's management of politics and policy in the second New Deal was thus the same as that during the Hundred Days. He focused the available political resources—his personality, popular support, respect for congressional prerogatives—into a unified strategy. One cannot single out any one element as crucial because all were complementary and, most important, congruent with the mood of the nation.

THE 1936 ELECTION AND THE FAILURE OF A THIRD NEW DEAL

Roosevelt approached the 1936 election campaign with continued reform on his mind and as his purpose. He had been angered by the actions of the Supreme Court against New Deal programs, and his relations with the business community had ruptured as organized opposition from that quarter mounted. His speech accepting the nomination threw down the gauntlet to the opponents of the New Deal as he promised "a war upon entrenched privilege" on behalf of a better life for all Americans. His campaign speeches appealed directly to farmers, workers, small business owners—all those who seemingly had been left out of the bankrupt capitalist consensus of the 1920s. In the final address of the campaign, he attacked the forces of selfishness and economic power and proclaimed, "I welcome their hatred." By September 1936, the polls showed him to be well ahead of Alfred Landon, the Republican candidate, so Roosevelt ran more on his previous policies than on any new departures. He won a great victory, carrying all but two states with almost 28 million votes against Landon's nearly 17 million.[27] Tugwell remembered that Roosevelt felt that such a reelection revealed that the American people had chosen him with a mandate to lead in the broad directions he had set out in the campaign.[28]

The campaign had been short on concrete proposals, however. The president had not advocated new programs with any specificity. He mistakenly took his personal victory to be tantamount to a blank check for policy. He privately thought that NRA planning should be revived in some form. He wanted wage-and-hour laws to protect working people. He also hoped for a program of rural resettlement, in which the urban unemployed would find work in the country. And he intended to create public authorities, like the Tennessee Valley Authority (TVA), in every major river valley. He was also frustrated with the obstacles that conservative Democrats in Congress had begun to erect against his programs, and began to think about how his party might be realigned as a liberal, reform party. Historians have suggested that a third New Deal, which would have been a combination of the first two, might have emerged. His second inaugural address sounded the trumpet when he said that the New Deal was not complete because "I see one third of a nation ill-housed, ill-clad, ill-nourished."[29]

Roosevelt intended to send far-reaching proposals in housing, agriculture, labor, and regional development to Congress, but he undercut his own objectives with a serious mistake. In February 1937, he surprised Congress and the country with a proposal to enlarge the membership of the Supreme Court from nine to a maximum of fifteen justices when any of the sitting justices reached the age of seventy and declined to retire. He tried to rationalize the reform in terms of the great workload on justices of greater age. This was a subterfuge, and everyone knew it. Roosevelt was angry at the Court decisions on the NRA and the Agricultural Adjustment Administration and feared that the Court might also declare unconstitutional Social Security, the TVA, and the Wagner Act, which strengthened collective bargaining. This imprudent action gave his political enemies a cause around which to unite and arouse the general public—Roosevelt as a dictator who wished to override the checks and balances of the Constitution. To aggravate the situation, the president then asked Congress for a thorough reorganization of the executive branch that would strengthen presidential authority over all departments and agencies, and which suggested possible attempts at national planning. Here was one more opening for attacks on the president as dictator.

On the evening before Roosevelt announced his plan for the Court, he asked Sam Rosenman to look over his message, which he had prepared without wide consultation. His mind was made up, but for the first time Rosenman noticed Roosevelt's nervousness and thought that it was very unusual for the president to be worried about a decision he had made. Rosenman perceived the president to be acting carefully but with great concern about the seriousness of the step he was about to take.[30] This time, the president had neglected to use his political antennae. This was apparent the next day, when Roosevelt read the message to his cabinet and the Democratic congressional leaders. He asked for no suggestions or advice, and no one volunteered. Vice President John Nance Garner and the congressional leaders did not say a word. Roosevelt then briefed the press about the proposal, having shown his press secretary the message only a few minutes earlier. The president had deliberately not consulted the Democratic congressional leaders for fear that they might try to stop him. He intended to increase public pressure on Congress by asking for the expansion of the Court before action was taken on his agriculture and wage-and-hour bills. The political rewards for members of Congress would come after they had done their duty on Court reform.

Roosevelt's miscalculation was disastrous for his presidency. As soon as the word was out, opposition rose from almost all the press and very strongly from Democratic congressional politicians. The Court-packing plan, justified in terms of age and workload, was clearly devious. Roosevelt had violated the central constitutional principle of separation of powers, and no matter what people thought of the Court and the New Deal, the principle was stronger.

The president eventually abandoned the artifice of expansion of the size of the Supreme Court and spoke directly to the public about the obstacles the Court had put in the way of the New Deal. He believed that a majority of Americans supported his position. But he failed. His own party in Congress would not defend him because public opinion did not agree with the president on the issue. Roosevelt was unable to present an argument against the Court that did not also violate the strong belief in the constitutional separation of powers.

The president's political weakness was clear for all to see in the aftermath of the Court fight when his proposal for the reorganization of the executive branch under increased presidential authority was spurned by Congress. The plan had not initially been controversial, but the Court fight permitted Roosevelt's critics to charge that the president wanted to be preeminent in government. All the opponents of the New Deal joined forces, and the president was able to secure only a modest administrative reform in 1939. He had twice been depicted by his enemies as violating the principles of American constitutional government. The president seemed to challenge traditional constitutional norms in favor of a claim to the superiority of presidential leadership.

These successful challenges to FDR showed that he could be beaten, and his political enemies took heart. The plans for a third New Deal were never tested because of the president's strategic errors. He had seemed invincible because of the large Democratic majorities in both houses of Congress. But not so. The president's defeat on the Court issue led to another great mistake. He declared war on the conservatives in his own party who had not supported his programs. He now wanted the Democratic party to be *the* liberal party. Early victories of two liberal southern Democrats in off-year elections had convinced him that it might be possible to defeat conservative Democrats who opposed New Deal programs, and he tried in Georgia, South Carolina, and Maryland. He personally spoke against three incumbent senators as being hostile to the New Deal and called for their defeat. He failed, thus illustrating the point that presidential approval is not easily, if at all, transferable. He did unseat one congressman from New York, but the purge was not regarded as successful. Sam Rosenman believed that the failure of the Court fight drove FDR to the equally rash error of the purge. And as with the Court battle, a presidential program is less compelling to voters than are constitutional principles—in this case, the autonomy of state and local electorates to elect their own representatives to Congress. FDR was vulnerable to the charge that he wanted to have a "rubber-stamp" Congress.

All in all, 1937 and 1938 were bad years for the president. In 1937 a group of conservative Democratic and Republican senators publicly stated their opposition to any further government infringement of "the American system of private enterprise and initiative."[31] The economy fell back into deep recession in 1937, and the president, who wished to spend federal money for relief work for the unemployed, persuaded Congress to raise taxes on the upper income brackets to pay for relief programs. This policy may have made the recession worse by taking money out of the economy just when greater spending and investment were needed. But the merits of deliberate deficit spending to achieve economic recovery were not yet understood. Roosevelt found himself caught between his own principles of budget balancing and the need for government to prime the spending pump. He embraced both in the absence of any theory that might override such a contradiction, and the failure was more intellectual than political. But a return to worse economic times hurt the president politically.

Why did Roosevelt, who was the very model of prudence, make such dramatic mistakes, one after the other, thereby weakening his presidency? He had exercised prudence during both the Hundred Days and the second New Deal, always carefully matching his leadership strategies to what he saw as the available political resources. Why did he misfire so badly in his second term? It is possible that he confused his great electoral victory, which was certainly a personal vindication, with a mandate to do whatever he wished. "I owe nothing to anyone," he said after the election. One consequence was that he consulted with congressional leaders much less than he had in earlier battles.[32] Rosenman remembered suggesting to the president that he talk more with the leaders in Congress, only to receive the reply that there was not time. Rosenman then commented that, in his view, the real reason was that FDR felt antipathy to those in Congress who had opposed him: he "hated to talk about government affairs with people who had offended him deeply or whom he disliked."[33]

Roosevelt was at his best as a bold, yet prudent, political leader when his abilities and the political environment reinforced each other. The task at hand had to appear achievable to him if he could put his talents fully to work. He saw the possibilities for success and carefully matched his strategies and tactics to those possibilities. Boldness was preceded by an analysis of limits. However, his victory in the 1936 election may have clouded his usual discernment. Prudence gave way to hubris. His very buoyancy and expansiveness were put to work without the prudence that was needed to temper them. The paradox is that he was most prudent when his skills were most challenged by the opportunity to achieve. He was less able to use his skills when he felt no constraint or when he felt himself to be unduly constrained. In the first instance, he indulged in hubris. In the second instance, he might act arbitrarily. In both cases, he lost his capacity for discernment. The positive relationship between skill and political environment is thus a dynamic one. Each element—personality and context—works on the other, so that the leadership that emerges is more forceful than it would be if based on either element alone. But this synergism was denied Roosevelt in 1937 and 1938 because he misread his environment and therefore was not stimulated to draw on his talent for coalition building.

There were other problems in Roosevelt's second term. The New Deal could not find a theory with which to bring economic recovery. Reform politics on behalf of the poor and unemployed may have lost its appeal. Roosevelt could not seem to find an issue on which he might exercise his great inventiveness to renew his presidency. He was depressed and seemed to some around him to be a "beaten man." But this was not to last for long.

❖ ❖ ❖

PREPARATION FOR WAR

Only toward the end of the decade did Roosevelt think it certain that the United States would be drawn into war. From 1933 to 1940, he worked to inform the nation of the danger of dictatorial governments in Europe and Asia; of the importance of an American buildup of military strength; and, after war began in Europe in 1939, of the need to aid the British and French in the hopes that American help would defeat Hitler without American intervention. He was working against a historical background of American isolationism in which the internationalism of Woodrow Wilson was thought to have failed. Therefore, his actions were cautious, were responsive to the moment, and at times appeared contradictory. As always, he felt his way, but he gradually developed a policy for "collective security" that was compatible with isolation. Americans were ready to admit by the mid-1930s that Hitler was a menace to peace, but it was very clear to Roosevelt that the public did not want the United States in a war. John Blum has captured the president's dilemma:

> For his part, the President during the 1930's shared the national reluctance to become involved again in a war in Europe. Nevertheless[,] anxious about the growing strength of the fascist countries, he was inclined, as a man of principle, to stronger action than he could undertake as president. The conflict between his personal impulses and his sense of political possibilities resulted in periods of caution and irresolution that no one in his situation could have avoided. Until 1940 he could not and did not take any effective step against aggression that depended upon congressional or public consent.[34]

Despite his passivity, Roosevelt did try to educate Americans about the dangers of the dictators and the necessity to improve military defense. And his political antennae were always at work. This was not the FDR of the Court fight and the purge. Neither was it the FDR of the first term, who could win by combining rhetoric and favorable politics. It was a president free of hubris who tried, over and over, to invent ways to educate the public and who continually fell short of his objective until war was forced on the United States. The hard question is whether Roosevelt pulled the nation into war by a series of incremental actions without the candor expected of a democratic leader.[35]

His own views on international relations were a blend of the realism of Theodore Roosevelt, who recognized the importance of national power in a lawless world, and the idealism of Woodrow Wilson, who envisioned the United States as the apostle of peace and law among nations.

The New Deal domestic programs had reflected the same tensions—between Hamilton and Jefferson, national power and dispersed government. Roosevelt brought these traditions together in American foreign policy, much as he had in domestic policy. But his realistic idealism was at variance with conventional opinion in the country. In particular, American progressives were convinced that an active foreign policy, with military implications, would mean the end of liberty at home. Roosevelt could do little as Europe moved toward war—the Italian invasion of Ethiopia, the Spanish Civil War, the German occupation of the Rhineland, the German annexation of Austria and of part of Czechoslovakia, and the Japanese invasion of China. Congress passed neutrality legislation that prohibited the American government from aiding any nation at war. It was easier for the president to try to be a peacemaker among nations, and he made several attempts, with no success.

After the Germans invaded Poland in 1939 and Britain and France entered the war against Germany, domestic public opinion was more favorable to the United States aiding the Allies, as long as it was not pulled into the war. Roosevelt used events, of which the public was aware, to teach. Neutrality laws were revised to permit the sale of weapons. The Nazi sweep across most of western Europe persuaded Americans of the need to strengthen the military. But in 1940 and 1941, the majority of the American public still wished to stay out of war. From the fall of France in 1940, Roosevelt moved step by step to help Britain. He traded old American destroyers for British bases in the Caribbean and, after his reelection in 1940, initiated lend-lease to Britain as a way to keep the United States out of war. But without the knowledge of the public, American naval operations in the North Atlantic were managed to protect British convoys and thwart German submarines. American merchant ships carrying supplies to Britain were armed. But it is not at all clear that the United States would have entered the war had not Japan attacked Pearl Harbor in December 1941. One could argue that the president provoked the attack by cutting off trade to Japan, particularly in oil, with the warning that trade would be resumed only if Japan withdrew from all its Asian conquests. This was not to be expected.

Was Roosevelt simply following and reacting to events? Or was he using events to manipulate public opinion? Or was he actually "teaching reality" to Americans? In the beginning, he simply tried to alert the public to the danger of dictators as an educational effort—for example, his 1937 speech in Chicago in which he recommended that the dictator nations be put in "quarantine." The speech was a reaction to the Japanese invasion of China. The public response was favorable, but only because the president drew no implications for an American military role. He disavowed any suggestions to the contrary in the face of congressional criticism. He had gone as far as he could go.

As soon as the Germans took all of Czechoslovakia in 1939, Roosevelt asked Congress to repeal the Neutrality Act of 1935, which it did. Public opinion had quickly shifted in favor of aid to Britain and France as a way of keeping the United States out of the war, which began in September 1939. The trading of British bases for destroyers was negotiated during the 1940 election campaign, and Roosevelt would not have been able to do it had not Wendell Willkie, the Republican presidential candidate, privately given his support. The president likewise persuaded a number of leading Republican foreign-policy leaders to say nothing. The American public was not told that the loss of the destroyers would weaken American defenses. Nor was it said to the public that the trade signaled the end of American neutrality.[36] However, a public-opinion poll revealed that 70 percent of the public supported the destroyer deal. Roosevelt had gone as far as he could have gone to aid Britain and yet keep the United States out of the war. He was forthright in the fall election campaign when he told an audience in Dayton, Ohio, that no combination of dictators could prevent the United States from helping the "last free people now fighting to hold them at bay."

But in September 1940, Willkie was lagging in the polls and broke with a bipartisan stance to attack Roosevelt as a warmonger. He deliberately tried to frighten people by telling them that their boys were sure to fight in Europe should FDR be reelected. The tactic worked, and Willkie's poll numbers began to rise. Roosevelt then began a series of speeches in which he denied any secret agreements and urged the importance of the military draft as a measure of defense only. On October 30, however, the latest Gallup poll showed Willkie only four points behind the president, and FDR decided to act boldly. He told an audience in Boston: "I have said this before, but I shall say it again and again and again. Your boys are not going to be sent into any foreign wars." He had said it before, but now dropped the line that had also been included: "except in case of attack." When he was reminded that he had always used this phrase in other speeches, he complained that it was unnecessary because we would obviously fight if attacked. Willkie's response was to say privately, "that hypocritical son of a bitch. This is going to beat me." And it did. Roosevelt won the election, but not by a large margin, getting 25 million votes to Willkie's 20 million.[37]

Congress had passed a military draft of one year in 1940, and a year later the military asked the president to ask for an extension of the period of service to two years so that the United States would continue to have an army. The military also wished permission to station draftees outside the Western Hemisphere, which had been prohibited by the law. The president asked Congress for the extension, but had to give way on service outside the hemisphere, and he won on the extension by only one vote in the House. Members of Congress were fearful of their constituents, with good reason, because polls revealed that a majority opposed service outside the hemisphere and a bare majority favored extension of the draft.[38]

Earlier in 1941, Roosevelt had responded to British pleas for help by inventing the lend-lease proposal under which the United States would sell, trade, lend, or lease military equipment to any nation whose defense was believed to be vital to American defense. The president was able to construct a coalition of progressive Republicans and Democrats and conservative Democrats to pass the law, but with very tight restrictions on presidential authority, particularly in the role of the navy as convoy to merchant ships. But in 1941, German submarines savaged British merchant ships, and the president moved on his own. He sent troops to Greenland and Iceland on behalf of American national defense, and he used executive orders "to repel any . . . acts of aggression directed against any part of the Western Hemisphere." Against Republican charges that he was denying the power of Congress to declare war, he cited his authority as commander in chief.[39]

By the fall of 1941, the president was anticipating entry into the war but would not ask Congress to declare war. He was waiting for a triggering event. Having used events to teach the public, he was dependent on new events. In September, he seized on an incident in which the American destroyer *Greer,* carrying passengers and mail to Iceland, was attacked by a German submarine. Later reports revealed that the *Greer* had been cooperating with a British patrol plane in tracking the submarine and that the plane had dropped depth charges on the Germans. Roosevelt ignored the facts and denounced the German action at a press conference and in a subsequent radio speech in which he called the German U-boats "the rattlesnakes of the Atlantic" and charged Germany with seeking the conquest of the Western Hemisphere. From now on, he said, American destroyers would shoot on sight to protect merchant ships. He was not honest with the public about the facts for fear that they would not support his plans for engagement. At that time, 80 percent of Americans opposed participation in the war, but in October, 70 percent told a Gallup poll that it was more important to defeat Hitler than stay out of the war.[40] But, ever cautious, the president took no risks. He wished both to break Hitler and to avoid war. Roosevelt feared that if he asked for a declaration of war, he would not get it and thus would lose any hold on opinion. Therefore, he led deviously by claiming that Germany was on a rampage in the North Atlantic, which was an exaggeration. Had he told the truth about the *Greer* incident, he could not have capitalized on it. This was a dangerous precedent for future presidents in the manipulation of public opinion, and it raises a fundamental question of democratic theory.[41] Teaching by events is one thing, but manipulating by distorting events is very different. Can the latter ever be justified by the national interest, and is the president the best interpreter of that interest?

The Japanese resolved Roosevelt's dilemma by attacking the United States, and Hitler obliged by declaring war. The fox was transformed into the lion, and a period of courageous war leadership began. But had Roosevelt intentionally moved the nation toward war, even though he justified each action as necessary to avoid it? This is a fair interpretation. But the president was following as well as leading.

He was feeling his way as much as the public, and what appeared, after the fact, to be manipulation may also be interpreted as the necessary dynamic of a democratic leader–follower relationship. Roosevelt's manipulations and distortions were not sufficient to pull the nation into war. Nor would he have used them for that purpose. He had to wait for events to unfold. Halford Ryan puts it well: "The public's reaction was motivated in part by FDR's rhetoric, just as his persuasive devices were a response to his audience's attitudes. By combining opinion polls with the practice of rhetoric, which in Roosevelt's case sometimes persuaded, sometimes reinforced, and sometimes failed, one can pronounce FDR a preeminent presidential persuader."[42]

❖ ❖ ❖

THE POLITICS OF AFFIRMATION

Franklin Roosevelt's greatest strength as a political leader was his great affirmation—of himself, of the American people, of the American story, and of hope for the future of the nation. He saw his own life and political career in the context of the unfolding of the progressive promise of American life. After all, he had known Theodore Roosevelt and Woodrow Wilson and had drawn much from both. His intuitions were alert to the emerging future, not in terms of a blueprint, but according to a blend of felt necessities and high ideals. He could be a trickster and loved manipulation, but such techniques were not sufficiently strong instruments for his purposes. His great ability to dramatize the choices that he presented to Americans was the key to his success. He was always cautious, but ever in terms of the idea of advancing. The sources of his talent for invention and dramatization were mysterious, even to himself, and certainly to his biographers. But that inventiveness was usually present when he needed it. The rhetoric of the first inaugural address, the principle of Social Security, the idea of lend-lease, and the United States as the "arsenal of democracy" were sparks of creativity.

To what extent did Roosevelt make a difference as president? World War II, rather than the New Deal, ended the Depression. The American party system was not realigned to make parties agents for coherent ideologies. His reform liberalism stayed within the limits of progressive principles. These were boundaries that no president could have crossed. He did make a difference as the agent of a new agenda for the role of government in the American polity. Progressivism was reinterpreted in ways that continue even today. He did teach Americans "the spirit of the constitution"; when he was seen to violate that spirit, he was rebuffed. This, rather than any particular legislative victory, was his great achievement. Finally, he knew how to fashion a coalition of interests in the country that was consistent with his over-arching progressivism. Neither the bully pulpit nor the concrete benefits would have been sufficient alone. He combined them.

Roosevelt was most effective as a political leader when he was required by politics to build coalitions by persuasion. His persuasive skills were brought out to their fullest in situations in which he had opportunities but no certainty of success. He could then "teach reality" and most often prevail because he provided plausible answers to ambiguous problems. His personal needs to be the center of attention and to lead were constrained by a healthy politics of persuasion. He failed when he cut himself off from political learning, as in the attempts to pack the Supreme Court and purge the Democratic party. The great potential flaw in his leadership was a grandiosity anchored in his buoyant egoism; he might fail to see the limits of possible action and overreach.

Roosevelt could misuse the powers of the presidency if institutions did not restrain him. This was clearly seen in his approach to impending war. He tried to educate, but he also manipulated to buttress the education. Leaders of such great talent are most effective when they work within institutional checks and balances. The American presidency requires it, but also leaves areas of discretion in which power may be abused. Therefore, our task is not solely to idealize FDR as an exemplar for democratic leadership, but also to ask about the conditions in which political talent is most effectively democratic.

5

Lyndon B. Johnson

❖ ❖ ❖ ❖ ❖ ❖ ❖ ❖ ❖ ❖ ❖ ❖ ❖ ❖

Politicians who aim to be president are extraordinarily ambitious. They possess the drive and tenacity to push on despite obstacles, setbacks, and disappointments. Their cardinal quality is that they never give up, as aspirants or as president. Most politicians seek attention, recognition, and success, however defined, but perhaps have no more or less drive and ambition than people at the top in the professions or business. There is a leap in kind beyond this sort of ambition to the drive of would-be presidents. This is not to say that all presidents are alike in their ambition. Franklin Roosevelt possessed a healthy narcissism in which he sought and accepted attention and love as virtually his birthright.

Lyndon Johnson was different. He was the central child in his family perhaps because of early recognition of his diverse talents. But his home life was not smooth, as Roosevelt's had been. His mother, who had married beneath herself in education and cultivation, placed Johnson in the vacuum his father, a rough and rustic politician, could not fill. And yet that love was made conditional on pleasing her. She could turn her back on her son if he did not act as she approved. He appropriated his father's masculinity and the world of politics, and combined them with an intense ambition for success that would please his mother. Johnson was not acting from strength so much as responding to emotional insecurity, which fed his enormous talents as one who must rule every group of which he was a member. There was a compulsive, unsatisfied character in Johnson's ambition that was not seen in Roosevelt's quiet tenacity. Johnson had to lay phantoms to rest.

He resisted attending college, but finally acceding to his mother's wishes, enrolled in San Marcos State Teachers College. There he began to display the political skills that were to characterize his public life. A position as assistant to the president of the school was converted into a virtual assistant presidency. He was a campus politician who, early on, showed that he knew how to build coalitions around himself. This kind of campus politician, who seems to be all knees and elbows, is seldom popular. Johnson was never popular as a politician. But he was awesome, his talents were on display, and people admired his talent and force of personality.

His talents were sharpened as a congressional aide, beginning in 1931; as the director of the National Youth Administration, a New Deal agency, in Texas in 1935 and 1936; and as a member of the House of Representatives from 1937 to 1948. He distinguished himself by his capacity for long days of hard work, by his willingness to drive his staff until they dropped, and by his assiduous cultivation of senior politicians in Washington and Texas who might help him up the ladder of ambition. But none of this was particularly spectacular. He did not have an opportunity to fully develop his talents until he became Democratic majority leader of the Senate in 1955.[1]

The Senate of the 1950s was made to order for Johnson's ability. It was a somewhat closed and comfortable "club" dominated by southern Democratic senators of long seniority who had placed themselves in key positions. Their doyen was Richard Russell of Georgia, whom Johnson adopted as his mentor, and who helped Johnson into first the minority and then the majority leadership in 1955.[2] Johnson had been elected to the Senate in 1948 with other remarkable men who made their mark on American politics: Hubert Humphrey, Estes Kefauver, Paul Douglas, Clinton Anderson, Robert Kerr, and Russell Long. They were all substantive experts and policy entrepreneurs, which Johnson was not. But he had the desire to lead and dominate the legislative process as a whole, which none of them had. The collegial character of Senate life, in which each senator was a king in his own eyes, was well suited to Johnson's political skills. He was never a man to nurture a deliberative process in which issues were openly debated, and then resolved by argument. His expertise was not in the substance of policy but in the management of people. He set himself the task of knowing the personalities and goals of every senator so that the final wording of a law would be the composite of many individually made bargains between himself and those whose votes were needed for passage. He did not like surprises and always wanted to know how a vote would come out in advance. If an outcome was anchored in tangible bargains, Johnson knew that he could prevail. He sought consensus and fled from confrontation.[3] As one biographer put it: "He incorporated the Senate into his own psychic processes, became inwardly absorbed by its mores, events and members, and took his obsession with him wherever he went."[4]

Johnson and Sam Rayburn, the Speaker of the House and an early mentor, were required by the facts of politics to cooperate with a popular president, Dwight Eisenhower, who was not a highly partisan Republican and with whom a legislative middle ground could be found. Johnson's greatest legislative achievement was his orchestration of Eisenhower's mildly reformist civil-rights bill of 1957 into law. This was admittedly accomplished by weakening the most muscular provisions of the original bill, but even so, it was a great achievement to overcome southern opposition and actually pass such legislation. The measure had passed the House, and most Senate Republicans supported it, in part, as a way of dramatizing Democratic divisions, North and South, on civil rights. The bill contained some teeth, which gave the Justice Department the authority to enforce civil rights guaranteed by the Fourteenth Amendment and provided for the prosecution of those who defied the law. Johnson made it clear to his own constituents and to southern senators that the bill, as written, was too strong; but, at the same time, he told Russell and other Southerners that civil-rights action, of some kind, was now inevitable, and the Senate had to act. A filibuster by southern senators might ensure the enactment of even stronger bills in the future. By endless discussions with all sides, he eventually found a way to pass a bill that gave lip service to a federal role in the enforcement of civil rights, but actually was more symbolic than effective. A frustrated president, who had hoped for more, signed the bill. But only Johnson could have persuaded southern senators not to filibuster, so that the bill, which eventually passed by a vote of seventy to eighteen, could get to the Senate floor. Johnson held his party and the Senate together and passed the first civil-rights bill since Reconstruction.[5]

Johnson had little understanding of and no sympathy for those senators who were critical of his style as majority leader because, under his leadership, conflicts were not resolved through open debate in which issues were joined. He believed that his method would produce results and that their approach would only guarantee deadlock. This was surely an accurate reading on his part of both national and Senate politics of the time. But Johnson's commitment to decisions by indirection and consensus was not just a tactical view; it was deeply rooted in his personality and style of leadership. Politicians play to their strengths, and he excelled at coalition building based on his knowledge of the many members of the potential coalition. He feared confrontation and polarization, in part because of his deliberate stance as a moderate between the two wings of his own Senate party. But he never liked confrontation at any time in his career. He wanted all parties to a deal to be satisfied not only with the deal, but with him. In later years, as president, he would spend hours trying to persuade those who disagreed with him on controversial issues to come around to his way of thinking. If they would not, he banished and derogated them. It was either all or nothing with Johnson. It was to be consensus on his terms. In this sense, he was a bargainer, but not really a persuader. If he could not bargain, he manipulated and intimidated. A subtle vein of coercion ran through his relations with others. In later years, he told Joseph Califano, a White House assistant, that "men are moved by love and fear, and the key to persuasion is to find the right measure of each to move them the way you want to."[6] He wanted to dominate, however he might do it. Much was made of the so-called

Johnson techniques of persuasion in which he used his powerful body and strong will to directly move his respondent. Certainly, his persona was an asset. But he was only part bully. He could also appeal to the idealism of others and to their deepest aspirations. But the one distinguishing characteristic of his persuasive powers was his reliance on his own skill and resources as fundamental to agreement. He was the key to everything, and nothing could be accomplished unless he was the leader.

Johnson had always wanted to be president simply because the White House was the top of the greasy pole. But his hope of being nominated for president in 1960 on the basis of his skills and achievements as Senate majority leader was not realistic. He could not match the campaign skills and popular appeal of John Kennedy. Just to be a very skilled Senate leader is not sufficient to be a viable presidential candidate. While Johnson was managing the Senate, Kennedy was running for president in the primaries. It surely became clear to Johnson that the only way he could ever hope to become president was to stand on a national stage, and in that sense, his acceptance of Kennedy's offer of the vice-presidential nomination was a highly rational decision.[7]

❖ ❖ ❖

FIRST YEAR AS PRESIDENT

Johnson succeeded to the presidency without having earned an electoral mandate. He therefore, naturally and logically, assumed that his mandate was to carry out Kennedy's ideas and plans. The theme of his first address to Congress was "let us continue." Thus he was able not only to build on the shock of Kennedy's death, but to assure the nation that the continuity and stability of government were ensured. His slow and dignified demeanor as he spoke to Congress was perfectly suited to the transition from an old to a new presidency. National grief gradually gave way to a national sense of restoration and confidence, and Johnson distinguished himself by his part in the continuing ceremony of passage out of grief.

He had always felt that he should not show his raw Texas side publicly, and suffered politically outside Texas as a result, because the sedate persona he presented was not the real Johnson and people knew it. But on the occasion of his assuming the presidency, the persona worked to achieve the intended effect.[8]

His legislative leadership in 1964 was extraordinarily forceful, however, as he worked to pass the main items of the Kennedy program: tax cut, civil-rights bill, and antipoverty program. A plan to cut taxes, according to Keynesian economic doctrine, as a means of stimulating a slack economy, had been introduced in Congress. The bill to outlaw racial segregation in public accommodations had passed the House and was facing a likely southern filibuster in the Senate. And what was to become Johnson's War on Poverty was still on the drawing board. Kennedy, with his lesser skills, might not have gotten all these measures through Congress, but Johnson did. His legislative skill was, however, helped by Kennedy's death and the ensuing mood of national unity. Johnson was thus able to lay the political foundation for the Great Society programs that came later when he became president in his own right.[9]

The chair of the Senate Finance Committee, Harry Byrd of Virginia, a conservative, was the first hurdle on the way to a tax cut. Johnson courted him by inviting him to breakfast at the White House, but, more important, made sure that the budget submitted for the new fiscal year came close to $100 billion, a symbolic threshold not to be exceeded. Byrd did not support the tax cut, but he let it pass to the floor for a vote. The cooperation of Secretary of Defense Robert McNamara, who had gotten a grip on the Pentagon budget, also helped in this respect. The president also reached out to business groups with the friendly message that as the economic pie grew, after a tax cut, conflicts among business, labor, and consumers would disappear. He wanted companies to make profits, he said, and he would never try to run their affairs. He brought his powerful natural persona to bear in meetings with the national leaders of business, and his appeals were so successful that, after the tax cut was signed in February 1964, *Fortune* magazine wrote: "Lyndon Johnson . . . has achieved a breadth of public acceptance and approval that few observers would have believed possible when he took office. . . . Without alienating organized labor or the anti-business intellectuals in his own party, he has won more applause from the business community than any President in this century."[10] Such a consensual political strategy was effective only as long as all the important, organized interests in the country, as well as the diffuse general public, were supportive of the president's goals.

Johnson found it necessary to pursue a different strategy for the passage of the civil-rights bill. He believed that such action was long overdue and had urged Kennedy to appeal to the "moral force" that black people in the South were demonstrating. He also knew that such a break with the past could not be effected by a legislative consensus, as had the tax cut. It was anathema to southern senators and their white constituents. But he also knew that if he did not lead on civil rights, "liberals" of all stripes would savage him. He decided not to bargain with Senator Russell, as he had done with the 1957 civil-rights law, but to beat the southern senators with Republican votes. He assiduously cultivated the Republican minority leader, Everett Dirksen, appealing to both the merits of the measure and the mark that Dirksen would make in history for having helped pass it. The appeal worked, and there were enough Republican votes to shut down a filibuster and pass the bill.[11]

Kennedy had asked his economists to develop ideas for an antipoverty program, and once Johnson learned of it, he immediately adopted it as his own. He very skillfully managed the politics of legislative passage by making a southern conservative Democrat the floor manager of the bill in the House. He met with many different groups favorable to such social action, making the same argument that he had made for the tax cut. As the economy grew and the size of the pie increased, it was only right to teach the poor new skills, through job training, with which to help themselves. This necessity of appealing broadly to a large audience meant that there was nothing radically redistributive in the bill. Political feasibility ruled that out. Again, it was consensus politics: all would benefit; none would lose.[12]

Polls in 1964 and 1965 showed very high public approval of LBJ as president, often as high as 70 percent. At the same time, the consensus leader had managed to make himself, as one historian put it, the "tribune of the liberals."[13] But the political masterstroke of August 1964, the passage of the Gulf of Tonkin Resolution, returned to haunt Johnson. An American destroyer supposedly had been attacked by North Vietnamese ships in neutral waters, and Johnson asked Congress to authorize him to use force to resist aggression in Southeast Asia. He was looking for an issue in the presidential election by means of which he might show the voters that he was just as tough on expansionist Communism as Barry Goldwater, who was talking fiercely about the possibility of strong American action in South Vietnam. The resolution strengthened Johnson on the militant side of the issue, after which he portrayed himself as the peacemaker and promised the voters that American boys would not fight Asian boys in Vietnam.[14] He was again the consensus leader.

❖ ❖ ❖

THE GREAT SOCIETY

Franklin Roosevelt and the New Deal had given Johnson his basic political identity, to which he added a strong infusion of southern populism. The objectives of the Great Society grew out of FDR's Economic Bill of Rights of 1944. Johnson had been in Congress since 1937 and knew how much more remained to be done and how important the president was in doing it. Whereas the later Roosevelt had been highly partisan, however, Johnson sought to unite all factions. He thought that the greatest presidents had been "men of reconciliation." He therefore avoided divisive rhetoric and in this regard was in harmony with the political climate of the day, in which American "pluralism" was celebrated and it was believed that political conflicts could be best resolved through bargaining.

The unusually large vote for Johnson in the 1964 election had given the Democrats 38 new seats in the House of Representatives, for a total of 295, so the votes existed to pass the president's programs. And the favorable economic and political climate was an important context for his success. Johnson's contributions to this situation were important but not crucial. Kennedy in a second term, after beating Goldwater, would have passed much of his program as well. But Johnson added two things. He knew how to involve key Democratic legislative leaders in the bills he sent down, so that passage was relatively smooth. And he pressed very hard for the enactment of as many bills as possible. He equated presidential greatness with quantity of achievement and wanted to be the greatest president ever. Wilbur Cohen, who worked for both Kennedy and Johnson at the Department of Health, Education and Welfare, later concluded that a Kennedy administration might have passed 125 bills instead of the 138 that Johnson drove through. Johnson also knew that his time for great legislative achievement was limited. At a White House meeting with all department legislative staffs in early 1965, Johnson told them that he would lose support every day by alienating someone by his actions. This had happened to both Wilson and Roosevelt. Therefore, he had to move fast to get his bills passed.[15] The irony was that, even after the Democrats lost seats in the midterm congressional elections of 1966, Johnson pressed for passage of bills right to his last day in office. Cohen remembered Johnson calling Senate Majority Leader Mike Mansfield and asking if it was possible to pass just one or two more bills on a given day. It was a numbers race for the president. But he also believed that he was being innovative. He relied on task forces of experts outside government to develop program ideas because he did not believe that regular bureaucrats could come up with fresh ideas. He also wished to establish himself with "the intellectual world."[16] He wanted scholars to write that he was a great president.

Walter Heller, who served as chair of the Council of Economic Advisers for both Kennedy and Johnson, remembered that Kennedy had actually become interested in the economic analyses presented to him, but that Johnson listened to his economists just enough to learn what his choices were, and then turned to the politics of the matter in question.[17] This was Johnson's role as ringmaster for the Great Society.

He made the key decisions about which program ideas to initiate and then orchestrated the politics of passage, delegating much to others, but always with a personal overview. He seldom got into the substance of policy, except as it affected political acceptability. Sam Hughes, a career official at the Bureau of the Budget, did not think that the big items—such as Medicare, federal aid to schools, and civil rights—involved difficult substantive issues. The tough part was getting political agreement, and Hughes regarded Johnson as far superior to other presidents he had worked for "in terms of knowledge, background, and so on in the Congress."[18] Califano remembered that the president would tell him to "go see [Senator] Wayne Morse—if he thinks it's ok, go forward. If he doesn't like it, it will die." One would not know what Johnson meant until the actual visit to Morse revealed Johnson to be accurately drawing on his long legislative memory.[19] Cohen remembered that Johnson relied heavily on people with whom he had had a long connection. He often knew what key members of Congress would accept because he knew their goals and values. Kennedy had been an outsider looking in at Congress, while Johnson acted as though he were still inside, looking out.[20]

The objective was consensus. To achieve it, Johnson, according to Cohen, relied on "triangulation," by which he elicited three or more sources of information on an issue. If all three agreed on the same course to be taken, Johnson moved ahead. He wanted agreement as a sign of achievement. As Cohen and others were working out a compromise about federal aid to Catholic schools, Johnson told him not to put him in the middle of a religious fight, with both the Baptists and the Catholics fighting him: "that's the primary thing I want you to keep in mind." The president's role was not to personally negotiate particular compromises with the principals, but to make sure that the politics of issues was kept under his close control. His central contributions to the enactment of programs were timing measures, in relation to one another; making sure that obstacles were removed in advance; and pushing hard for passage. The impact of this kind of political skill on the actual passage of bills cannot be assessed quantitatively. The larger than usual number of Democrats in Congress was surely a prerequisite for action. But Johnson brought the same skill to the process that had been successful in 1964 with fewer votes. And this skill was employed almost entirely with small bands of people rather than with the larger public. He had the votes in Congress; there was no need to return to the well of public opinion. He was most effective with appeals to particular groups. For example, Douglas Cater, a White House assistant, remembered LBJ's persuasiveness with the leaders of the American Medical Association about his determination that Medicare pass: "I've seen him take groups like that and almost mesmerize them. He had the capacity, which he developed over long years of trying to bring together hostile groups in Congress, of combining all his charm, all of his eloquence, shrewdness, to overpower a group like that."[21]

He deliberately pitted advisers against one another, even within his immediate staff, which produced friction and conflict, but also enabled him to learn. He had a passion for keeping options open on a new policy idea until, as Califano said, "every political stone was turned." White House aides could speak frankly to him.[22] This is an important point to make because Johnson was later accused of manipulating his associates in order to hear only what he wished to hear about the Vietnam War. He may have done so in regard to the substance of policy, but in both domestic and foreign policy his search for political pitfalls and eventual agreement was always strong. He was confident that he understood politics, and he played to this strength. It served him well in domestic policy but not so well in foreign policy, where he was less comfortable with both policy and politics.

This is not the place to recount the legislative achievements of the Great Society. The federal government assumed a large number of unprecedented commitments in health, education, and welfare, most of which were not reversed by subsequent presidents. Johnson believed in all of it. His principal role was political orchestration. But his leadership in civil rights was extraordinary and was one of the few issues he took to the public. It took courage and a commitment to principle over politics. After he signed the Civil Rights Act of 1964, he told Bill Moyers, his chief policy assistant at the time, "I think we delivered the South to the Republican party for your lifetime and mine."[23] But Johnson thought it right to press ahead despite the political costs. His actions on behalf of the Voting Rights Act of 1965 prove it. Police had run down and manhandled a group of civil-rights marchers in Selma, Alabama, who were on their way to the state Capitol to petition for the right of blacks to vote, and the scene had appeared on national television. Johnson seized the moment to also appear on national television, in a nighttime address to Congress, on behalf of the voting rights bill. He told his fellow politicians that the right to vote is guaranteed in the Constitution for all Americans, that he intended to make sure that no one was denied that right, and that he hoped they would help him. He finished his speech with the slogan of the civil-rights movement: "We shall overcome."[24] This was authentic leadership in which Johnson expressed his beliefs and reminded others of their necessary commitments. It may also be the case that he thought that a Democratic president who would be great must lead on civil rights. His place in history was never far from his mind. Johnson was capable of moral leadership and exercised it in this instance, but he was seeking consensus, even here, by insisting that all should agree on the right thing to do. His leadership for the Great Society, while suffused with bargaining, also implicitly appealed to national agreement on the needs of the nation. All hinged on the maintenance of consensus, but it was not to be.

THE EROSION OF THE GREAT SOCIETY

The New Deal coalition built by Roosevelt continued as a political force long after its programmatic fires had burned out. Johnson rekindled the fire but, in the process, undermined the bases of the old coalition. He asked the satisfied groups in that coalition, especially white working people, to support action on behalf of the dispossessed and poor that eventually appeared to affect their jobs, housing, and values negatively.[25] Johnson's social programs reflected less a fresh, new coalition of support in the country than his own strong will and desire for greatness. The Roosevelt New Deal had been grounded in concrete constituencies—workers, farmers, minorities, the unemployed, people whose lives had been dislocated by the Depression. Johnson, in contrast, aimed his programs at the bottom of society and hoped that the rest of the country would follow. Paul Conkin has called this a "politics of moral complacency," in which the better off are asked to help the worse off just for goodness' sake.[26] But consensus politics was too shallow. In the last two years of his presidency, Johnson faced the white populist revolt of George Wallace on his right, which had great appeal to white working people, and the "new politics" of militant blacks and radicals on his left. The New Deal coalition was breaking apart because of the strains that Johnson had imposed on it.[27]

The rioting of urban blacks in large cities in the summers of 1966 and 1967 not only cut the heart out of the credibility of the civil-rights movement, but disillusioned many whites about civil-rights programs. This became even more biting when whites and blacks began to compete for jobs in greater numbers. Johnson had counted on economic growth to increase resources sufficiently to fund his social programs without harming the economy. But trying to fight a war without paying for it, through either increased taxes or reduced domestic budgets, neither of which Johnson would willingly do in 1966 and 1967, put great strains on the grand safety net he had erected.[28] The only way the country could support both guns and butter was through inflation or tax increases. Even so, the Great Society programs were subjected to spending reductions, and congressional leaders held Johnson hostage to his refusal to cut social programs significantly in return for a tax increase.[29] By 1966, Johnson's pressure on employers and unions to keep wages and prices down had failed. His refusal to recommend a general tax increase to Congress in early 1966, against the advice of his economists, eventually came back to haunt him. Johnson had concealed the projected cost of the Vietnam War from the public because he had gambled on a short war and had lost.

There was another reason for Johnson's loss of credibility over the Great Society. He had promised too much and delivered too little.

There was too little spending on the new programs for too short a time, despite the great gains made by many. Califano felt that the president had overestimated the capacity of government to administer the many new, complex programs. Califano and his small number of colleages in the White House spent hours and days, on the orders of the president, meeting with department heads and trying to resolve conflicts among their bureaucracies at the grassroots level, where the programs were implemented. John Blum argued that Johnson's grandiosity crippled the government, which was not prepared for such massive administrative tasks.[30]

Johnson had no political coalition of his own to counter the fissures within his consensus vision. However, it is too easy to say that he should have been a more radical leader with a popular coalition to match. There was no such coalition, nor could there have been. There was no depression. Times were good. The political success of the Great Society was a luxury that could not endure if economic problems appeared, which they did. Johnson was a prisoner of the consensus, but so was all liberal politics.

The president's personal unpopularity grew in bounds after 1966, and he had nothing to tell the public beyond what he had already said. He was not able to win passage of the tax increase that he had eventually sought until after he withdrew from the presidential race in 1968. These domestic problems were intensified by the prosecution of the war in Vietnam, and for a full understanding of the pathos of Johnson's fall we must look there.

VIETNAM

In March 1964, in recorded telephone conversations with Secretary of Defense Robert McNamara and Senator William Fulbright, chair of the Senate Foreign Relations Committee, Johnson expressed his uncertainties about what the United States should do in defense of its ally South Vietnam. On March 2, he told Fulbright that he favored the

United States maintaining the present course of military support for the government of South Vietnam without a fighting role. The hard question, he said, would come in the future if that policy failed and it was either fight or get out. He set out three options to McNamara that might be presented to the American public: send in American troops to fight; get out and let the Vietcong guerrillas swallow up South Vietnam; keep teaching the South Vietnamese how to fight so that they might defeat the Vietcong. He thought the third choice was the best for the moment. If that failed, he said, then another decision would have to be made, but it had not yet failed.[31] These conversations were probably a good guide to Johnson's thinking at that time. The questions were implicitly framed by the ideology of containment of Communism, which had been the operative theory of American policy makers since 1947. The successive commitment of all presidents since Truman to resistance to Communist expansion in Southeast Asia, especially Indochina, was clearly shared by Johnson and his advisers. They believed that South Vietnam not only was strategically important to the support of the rest of Southeast Asia, but was an American commitment that had to be honored. The decisions that were to follow in 1964 and 1965 to escalate the American military role were all tactical, without any fundamental inquiry into the premises that underlay them.[32] All of Johnson's beliefs were from the political mainstream, and the American commitment to South Vietnam was part of that mainstream and one piece of Johnson's strong commitment to continuity with the policies of the Kennedy administration.

Containment was an example of the liberal realism that characterized American foreign policy during the Cold War as a reaction against the supposed innocence of Wilsonian peacemaking after World War I. Realism grew out of the lessons of appeasement of the 1930s. Aggressors must be faced down as they acted. Otherwise, they would continue to move forward. Thus the use of military force, in such a good cause, was justified. We will ask, as the analysis proceeds, whether liberal realism was sufficiently realistic about the pitfalls of fighting a limited war in Southeast Asia in defense of an ally that would not fight for itself.

We must also understand the politics of foreign policy that had accompanied containment theory in order to place Johnson in the context of the political costs and benefits of his choices as he understood them. The Truman administration had been scarred politically with responsibility for the "loss" of China to the Communists in 1949. The spread of McCarthyism among Republican politicians was the consequence. Democrats were driven to prove that they were not "soft on Communism." The stalemate in the Korean War reinforced this politics as the action became "Truman's war." And yet, in retrospect, Korea was thought to be a successful example of how to fight a limited war without risking a wider conflict. Johnson believed that if he were to be charged politically with the "loss" of any nation to Communism, he would have difficulty getting any of his social programs through Congress. But he also must have known that limited wars are not popular with Americans unless they are brief and victorious. The Korean War had denied Truman the opportunity to run for reelection had he wished to do so. The dilemma facing Johnson had sharp horns.

The gradual escalation of the American role in Vietnam in 1965, culminating in July in the decision to send ground troops to fight, appears to have come about by a process of incremental choices made by the president and his lieutenants without any one seriously considering the possibility that there was less at stake than had been assumed or that the odds of success were very low. The "price of consensus" according to Leslie Gelb and Richard Betts, was "a middle road of contradictions and no priorities for action."[33] There had been no such analysis in either the Eisenhower or the Kennedy administration. The question of whether the South Vietnamese could defend themselves was never faced. As one unstable regime succeeded another in South Vietnam, American policy makers became prisoners of their commitment to a government that was only a vacuum; yet this did not matter because the real issue was American credibility. South Vietnam had to be saved in spite of itself. There was no evident hubris or belief that the United States could prevail easily. The president and his advisers were gloomy, but they would not consider the possibility of withdrawal. They still believed in the domino theory, which was an application of containment doctrine.[34] There were a few devil's advocates. Senator Mike Mansfield, an expert on Asia, read a memo to the Johnson inner circle opposing the escalation of the war, but the president did not encourage discussion. Undersecretary of State George Ball predicted that American assumption of the war would be a disaster in which the military would become trapped without any possibility of winning. Johnson listened carefully, but Ball could not give the president a politically feasible way to get out of Vietnam. Secretary of State Dean Rusk wrote a memo to the president that presented the American stake in Vietnam as a matter of credibility of its commitments. This argument was moral rather than empirical; indeed, the dismaying empirical situation could make no difference to such a thesis. The United States could not abandon its commitments. Even Ball agreed that withdrawal was unacceptable, telling the president that he was on board no matter what decision Johnson made.

Finally, in June 1965, it became clear to all that the bombing in Vietnam had not achieved the purpose of bringing the Vietcong and North Vietnamese to negotiations. General William Westmoreland, the commander of American forces in South Vietnam, requested a large infusion of American troops, not only to defend American installations from attack, but to fight. Johnson was at the fork in the road where he had hoped never to be. We know what he did, but why did he do it and was there any alternative that could have freed him from what appeared to be a no-win situation?[35]

Historians and political scientists will never be able to definitively explain why Johnson acted as he did. It is the nature of historical explanation that known facts are necessarily reinterpreted by fresh insights. But there may be sufficient evidence to estimate the balance between purpose and prudence in Johnson's thinking. Three broad hypotheses cover the possibilities:

1. Johnson and his advisers were Cold Warriors who believed in containment theory, falling dominos, and the American obligation to the government of South Vietnam.

2. Johnson believed that the failure to act in defense of South Vietnam would create intense domestic political warfare such that the Great Society programs, which were just moving in Congress, would be stopped.

3. Both of the previous explanations are valid, but the real problem was Johnson's style of authority, in which, as a legislative kind of leader, he sought consensus among his advisers and would not ask for careful analysis of policy choices that might have broken that consensus.

These hypotheses are not mutually exclusive. The evidence is clear that all the decision makers, except Mansfield and Ball, believed that the American commitments in the Cold War were on the line in Vietnam. Johnson saw China and the Soviet Union as bent on domination of the region and believed that he could not allow that to happen. Johnson was evidently less concerned with negative public opinion should he fail to act forcefully to strengthen the American commitment, than with the possibility that right-wing politicians would charge him with a defeat in the Cold War. This, in turn, might create such a partisan conflict with the Republicans that the Great Society programs would be lost. At the time of Johnson's decision in July to send ground troops to Vietnam, Medicare was in a Senate–House conference and other important bills were awaiting final action. This is the favorite conventional explanation of escalation. Johnson wanted both the Great Society and a limited war and was faced in June and July with the choice of either escalating the war or possibly losing the Great Society. This theory is very plausible. It also helps explain why so little fanfare was given to the decision to send more troops.

The third hypothesis does not deny the validity of the other two, but suggests that Johnson might have saved the Great Society and his presidency had he asked for more careful analysis of the options not taken in Vietnam and the perils of those chosen. The incremental decision making of late 1964 and the first half of 1965 was marred first by the failure to face the realistic prospects that might be achieved by bombing, and then, when bombing failed, by the inability to turn back. The hard questions had never been asked; when crisis erupted, there was no time to ask them.[36] The most persuasive argument is less Johnson's lack of understanding of policy analysis than his style of authority. He acted as president as though he were still a leader of the Senate—covering all the political bases and getting all dissenters on board. This was the way he had worked as president in 1964 and 1965, with great success. Why should he change?

A purely psychological explanation of Johnson's decision, as welling from his personal insecurity and his fear of disapproval of his Kennedy advisers, particularly Robert Kennedy, is not convincing as a major explanation. There were too many other good political reasons to explain his actions. It remains the case, however, that his search for consensus in decisions, dislike of outsiders, and fear of open conflict, all of which characterized his entire political career, had deep roots in his personality.[37]

Considering all the facts, it appears that everything about Johnson and the situation in which he found himself allowed him very little freedom to act other than as he did. The layers of motivation all pointed in the same direction: preserve continuity with the Kennedy administration, adhere to conventional Cold War beliefs, avoid the kind of political bitterness that a withdrawl might cause, and hope for a short war that would not imperil the Great Society. It would have taken a very different sort of political leader and president to have challenged the consensus of his advisers and created political support in Congress and the country for withdrawal from Vietnam. The regime would surely have fallen. The American people, who knew nothing about the place, might not have cared. But a president who so acted probably would have had a big partisan fight on his hands. This was not Johnson's style. He abhorred conflict. One can only ask, but not answer, why he did not remember more carefully Truman's loss of support for a war that could not be won, especially since Johnson pursued the same middle way, with exactly the same result. This concern was perhaps not strong enough in light of the choices that Johnson had to make in July to have been anything more than a latent fear. He wanted to lead all the nation, and going forward in Vietnam seemed the best way to do that.

The president called congressional leaders of both parties to explain his decision to send more troops to Vietnam and met with general support. Even Senator Richard Russell, who had always been skeptical of the Vietnam commitment, told Johnson that now that the United States had become so involved, it had to finish the job. Leading columnists and the attentive public also supported the president at this time, and public opinion in general stayed with the effort for considerable time after that.[38] Johnson did not tell the public about the extent of American military actions in Vietnam in 1965, nor did he go directly to the public to explain his decision. McNamara and the Joint Chiefs of Staff urged the president to declare a national emergency, call up the reserves, and, if necessary, ask Congress for additonal taxes. The president refused, saying that he had the constitutional authority to act and that he feared that militant politicians on the right would press for a greater military effort, which might bring the Chinese and Soviets into the conflict. Johnson followed Truman's middle-of-the-road tactic and suffered the same fate. He could not "lose" South Vietnam, but he would not fight a wider war. Therefore, he feared to speak to the public in militant tones. He made restraint the key to his policy and saw himself as a moderate who held all the war dogs in check.[39]

The problem with this posture was that Johnson was never able to persuade an increasingly skeptical public that the military effort in Vietnam was worth the costs. A long, frustrating war that seemingly could not be won undermined the president's credibility with the public. It is difficult to separate Johnson's deluding the public from his failure to be honest with himself. By late 1966, according to Califano, the "credibility gap" was destroying Johnson's presidency. An increasing number of Americans simply did not believe that the war was going well or was winnable. Unrealistically low administration defense budgets and unduly optimistic reports on how the war was going widened the credibility gap. Califano believed that Johnson denied the facts of military failure. As public criticism of the war increased, the president retreated into his shell and refused to listen to critics; doubters in his own house, including Bill Moyers, even McNamara, were sent away.[40] Vice President Hubert Humphrey was barred from meetings until he became a public advocate of the American commitment to South Vietnam. Johnson could understand himself only as the leader of a consensus. He was no different from how he had been as Senate leader; those who challenged his way of managing business were a threat to business itself. Johnson had contempt for critics of the war, much as he had been critical of Democratic senators who did not like the way he manipulated consensus in the Senate.

In Johnson's last two years as president, much of the public came to believe that the American commitment in Vietnam was a mistake. There was no clear position on what to do about it, but confidence in Johnson declined; in late 1967, only 28 percent of the public approved of his handling of the war.[41] Opinion was divided between a smaller number who would withdraw from Vietnam and a larger number who would escalate the military effort, and Johnson gradually learned that his middle way was not working. In early 1968, the North Vietnamese armies attacked all over the south in an effort to finish the war with a military victory. The Tet offensive failed, but the pictures of destruction on American television were a shock to those who could see no hope in more of the same American effort. Political management of the war had required "manufacturing a world of appearances," and the Tet offensive revealed the deception. In the New Hampshire presidential primary election in 1968, in which Johnson barely defeated Senator Eugene McCarthy, it was clear that Johnson had become the scapegoat for a very unpopular war.[42] He had suffered the fate of Harry Truman, who also had been weakened by an unfavorable New Hampshire primary in 1952.

Johnson gave up the presidency when he realized that he could not maintain consensus on the Vietnam War. His own advisers, official and unofficial, were now telling him that the war could not be won and that he must find a way out through negotiation. This provided an opportunity for him to once again be a consensus leader. He agreed to a new peace iniative and withdrew from the presidential race to impress the North Vietnamese that politics would not interfere with the search for peace. He could be the statesman again.

❖ ❖ ❖

PURPOSE AND PRUDENCE

G. K. Chesterton believed that great leaders must be men who are "sturdy enough to endure and inflict brutality" because in the process they are also "sturdy enough to alter it."[43] Johnson was that kind of man. His very lack of a sense of limits was a great strength in his drive to accomplish the impossible. But it was also a trap that he would unwittingly set for himself again and again.

The historical context was favorable to Johnson's leadership in civil rights and social policy. He knew how to accommodate his political abilities to social currents. His ambition was a powerful engine for good. Wilbur Cohen thought that Johnson had a "sense of history" in which "he wanted to be a great president. . . . He didn't want to be an ordinary president." But "he wanted to do more than a human being could possibly do," with the result that the American people could not handle so much change in one time. But his ambition required him to push and achieve.[44]

Many of the social programs of the Great Society had a major flaw: they were enacted so quickly that little thought was given to their implementation. Johnson was not interested in such questions, and thus they were buried in his haste for action.[45] And when the inevitable political backlash came, he dismissed his critics as ungrateful and ignorant. He was not capable of admitting that the programs themselves might be flawed or that new policy questions had been uncovered by ragged implementation. Califano understood that Johnson "wanted to control everything" and got angry at people or situations he could not control, in both small and large matters.[46]

Had Johnson's presidency been primarily one of leadership for domestic policy, he might have adjusted to the political backlash against his programs. But he was as defensive about these programs as he was about the American commitment in Vietnam. We can only speculate whether he could have learned and adapted to different domestic tasks. The war did not give him the opportunity. His style of authority was exactly the same in peace and war, but his intensity and defensiveness were multiplied in the latter.

But we must not convict Johnson as solely responsible for mistakes in regard to Vietnam. His advisers were united, and congressional leaders and the public initially supported his decisions, which were in keeping with established presidential policy from Truman's time. It has been argued that no other president would have tried to implement a wide-ranging social program and conduct a war at the same time. The problem perhaps was not in trying to do both, but in trying to do both with such intensity. Johnson had a keen sense of limits as Senate majority leader, but he knew the politics of the chamber, which did not require him to understand national politics well. When he became president, his sense of limits was necessarily attenuated by the larger number of actors in his political world, many as far away as Southeast Asia.

Johnson's great failure as a political leader was that he did not understand deliberation. He understood only control. He wanted consensus, but only the consensus that he could manufacture by manipulation. He lost control, though, and hubris was followed by depression and defensiveness, about both domestic and foreign policy. He was afraid of open deliberation, either in his own counsels or in public. And because he was the manipulator of the consensus, he inevitably became the scapegoat when opposition to his policies developed. His scapegoating of others turned back on itself. His exercise of power consumed his authority.

None of this is to say that the United States would not have tried a fighting role in Vietnam or that the result would not have been as tragic as it was. It is to say that the special intensity that Johnson gave to all his actions was unable to foster a climate of deliberation in which policies might have been examined more carefully and commitments made less quickly. His ambition was too strong for his limited sense of prudence. The more fundamental point is that his style of authority was not well suited to the requirements of a deliberative democracy. In this sense, Lyndon Johnson compares unfavorably with Franklin Roosevelt.

6

Ronald Reagan

❖   ❖   ❖   ❖   ❖   ❖   ❖   ❖   ❖   ❖   ❖   ❖   ❖   ❖   ❖

Ronald Reagan is an American Adam who has always believed in the innocence and goodness of the American promise. He believes that the promise can be fulfilled because nothing is impossible to Americans by virtue of who they are. His world of aspiration, despite the power of his vision, is also a world of illusion. He consistently romanticized his own experiences as he honed them for the political rhetoric of promise and innocence. His boyhood was spent in the seemingly idyllic small-town life of the Middle West, but his family moved ten times as his father pursued a shaky selling career; the father, although loved by his family, was an alcoholic. Reagan's mother was, by all accounts, a nurturing and loving woman who urged her two sons to love their father. Children respond in many ways to alcoholism in parents, so the kind of child and youth that Reagan became cannot be explained by his father's problems. One can point to early characteristics, however, to which Jack Reagan's alcoholism probably contributed. The son did not discuss his feelings with others, as child or adult. He developed an optimism that seemed to contain elements of denial of the darkness of life. He became absorbed in the amateur theatrical world of his mother and performed in plays, in church and school, that she wrote for him.[1]

Two college successes surely shaped the aspirations of the young

Reagan as he learned what he could do well. He took part in a student strike against the president of Eureka College as a designated spokesman for freshmen. Although he was only one of many student leaders, his later accounts distorted the story to make him the single hero of the successful strike. His role in the strike, as he remembered it, permitted Reagan to attack authority in the name of the tradition of the college. He was a leader in a conformist rebellion. And the episode could be retrospectively dramatized as a morality play in which good and bad clashed.[2]

The second success was the high point of his college acting career, when he won an award for a performance at Northwestern University and was encouraged by the director of the Northwestern drama program to pursue an acting career. He accepted this advice, as he later said, in "stunned ecstasy."

Reagan was president of his high-school and college student bodies, but his acting experiences directed him toward entertainment rather than politics. He wanted to be a sports announcer in the manner of a number of talented radio personalities. He was determined to get out of the small-town Midwest, even though he was always to idealize it in his memory. He was to seek wider and wider stages on which to perform for the rest of his career.

As a sports announcer in Des Moines, Reagan taught himself to use his voice to generate excitement among listeners. There were many examplars among proficient radio announcers, but the most proficient teacher was in the White House talking to the nation in brief radio addresses in a calm and reassuring manner. The day of the "shouter" was over.[3]

The ambitious young man broke into Hollywood movies just at the time that producers at the big studios were competing to present idealized versions of American life. Reagan was superbly suited for portraying the American "everyman" through a medium that combined new technology with traditional social values and norms. The message was reassuring even as the medium was radical. The language of individualism was conveyed in an "other-directed" entertainment milieu. The irony of Reagan's movie career was that he was unsuited for the heroic action parts he wanted. He could not be John Wayne, but he was very good at light comedy.[4] His failure to understand the nature of his talent may have contributed to the decline of his movie career after World War II.

Numerous biographers of Reagan have shown how he later incorporated movie stories into his own mental and psychological world and used them for political effect. His frequently repeated story about the bomber pilot who chose to ride a plane down with a trapped gunner rather than bail out could, of course, not be confirmed. It may have been a scene in a movie. But that criticism misses the point. Literal truth mattered less to Reagan than symbolic meaning. Reagan was not unique among politicians in dramatizing issues with exaggerated narratives. He was different, however, in his capacity to apply Hollywood mythmaking to the service of political leadership.[5]

His experience in the 1950s as a spokesman for General Electric gave him the opportunity to perfect his speaking abilities before live audiences in the GE plants. He repeatedly gave the same speech that he was to deliver for the rest of his career. The message was pro–free enterprise, anti-Communist, and antigovernment. He learned, through trial and error, just which themes would work best with an audience of average Americans. He was a very calculating performer in his ability to observe the effect of his techniques and words on others. To him, these appearances were everything, and he conserved his time and energy during his tours of the plants to make sure that he had plenty of practice and rest before he spoke. This attention to the speaking role as the most important one for him was to characterize his governorship and presidency.[6]

Reagan made the transition from liberal Democrat and supporter of Roosevelt and Truman to conservative Republican during the years that Eisenhower tacitly accepted the New Deal on behalf of "modern" Republicans. One result was that Reagan became the logical spokesman for the conservative movement in Republican politics after the debacle of Barry Goldwater's run for the presidency. His televised and widely distributed speech for the Goldwater campaign made him appear to be a more reasonable person than Goldwater, who was given to extravagant statements. Reagan, the actor, knew how to underplay his lines in a relaxed and nonthreatening manner, even as the ideas were starkly conservative.[7]

GOVERNOR

As a candidate for governor of California, Reagan was initially hopeless. He had little knowledge of issues and would pop off with ill-considered ideas without restraint. As a result, he was required to submit to a team of consultants who taught him how to avoid verbal missteps, educated him on issues, and controlled his schedule to give him enough time to rest and prepare for his performances. His campaign against the incumbent governor, Pat Brown, focused on moral and symbolic issues, causing the Brown camp to underestimate Reagan's threat. They saw their opponent as a failed actor, amateur politician, and right-wing ideologue who easily could be beaten. This mistake was made by all of Reagan's subsequent political opponents. Reagan's rhetoric in 1966 appealed to middle- and working-class suburbanites who resented high taxes and government aid to minorities. They said they wanted less government, but wanted to continue those programs from which they benefited. Reagan played to this wish beautifully. He presented himself as a "citizen politician" and made Brown the scapegoat for all of California's problems: the Berkeley student unrest, the Watts riots, and so on. He was the apostle of hope who promised Californians that it was within their power to begin the world anew.[8]

Reagan was served by excellent staff assistants in his two terms as governor and followed their direction to play his part as public articulator of purpose. He could make decisions if the alternatives were presented in an orderly way, and he was not afraid to take bold steps, such as the firing of the president of the University of California. His rhetoric described how California government was being turned in a conservative direction, but the actual policies were only modestly conservative. He would not let reality intrude on rhetoric, nor would he allow his public language to get in the way of the necessities of government.[9] He raised taxes when the state faced a serious budget deficit and then claimed that the subsequent unanticipated surpluses were the result of budget cutting. He attacked big government rhetorically, even as he learned to accommodate himself to his department heads and praised the accomplishments of his administration. He said later that the most important thing he had learned as governor was that he could work with a Democratic legislature. In his governorship, Reagan showed that he had the ability to win the support of citizens for his values and aspirations rather than his actual accomplishments. He was very talented at the politics of interpretation. It must be added that he seldom acted to scale back popular programs. He consolidated as he preached renewal.

Reagan had always been more interested in national than in state issues and had set his eyes on the White House from the start. He planned to be a decisive governor in his first year and use that record in a run for the presidential nomination in 1968. But Richard Nixon's comeback was too strong.[10] Reagan almost took the nomination away from Gerald Ford in 1976, and as he prepared to run again in 1980, the country seemed to have grown more conservative in the sixteen years since Goldwater's failure. High inflation, setbacks in Iran and Afghanistan, resentment at the misfiring of the Great Society programs, and the seeming weakness and ineffectiveness of Jimmy Carter's presidency—all played into Reagan's hands at the same time so he was able to persuade voters that he would be a responsible leader in office.

❖ ❖ ❖

POLITICAL PERSONALITY

Reagan brought a fully developed style of leadership to the presidency. His operational code had been tested by experience, and it was to guide him for the next eight years. His rhetorical skills were foremost, but it would be mistaken to depict him as pandering to public opinion. Rather, he invoked cultural themes in which he strongly believed and which he knew, from trial and error, would be popular. He had the ability to be himself, to be authentic, and yet to appeal to the concerns of others.[11] He was perfectly suited to a period of resentment because his stock-in-trade had become the promise to restore neglected values and redirect government without being radical about it. The resentments to which he appealed were more symbolic than substantive. As Lou Cannon, who covered him for eight years, remembered, Reagan liked people, but he also "practiced to do those things that people liked."

His personal style as an executive was congruent with his rhetorical style. He was content to be managed by others, much as an actor is managed by directors, as long as he was free to speak to the few basic themes that were so important to him. Both his executive and his public styles of leadership were accompanied by an extraordinary detachment from the concrete. He was always courteous to and affable with assistants, but seemed to care little for them as individuals. He would not attempt to manage and resolve personal conflicts, whether in his private or his official families.[12] He was seldom knowledgeable about the specifics of his own policies or about the work of government. He was a dramatist and thus lived to a certain extent with illusion. Preaching a vision was his vocation.

It would be inaccurate to depict Reagan as a soft, amiable demagogue who simply wished to be liked, however. His longtime aide Michael Deaver remembered that those assistants who underestimated or belittled Reagan did not survive. Cannon believed him to have "a hard, self-protective core that contained both a gyroscope for maintaining balance and a compass pointing toward success." Reagan had relentlessly pursued his political ambition into ever-widening circles throughout his career, and his amiability, which concealed the ambition, caused opponents and even friends to underestimate him. Thus any analysis of Reagan's talents as a politician must recognize that he always was more than he seemed to be to his detractors and less than he seemed to be to his partisans. He was a very difficult man to know.

ELECTION

By 1980, the public had given up on Jimmy Carter. He appeared to have lost control of events.[13] And, just as important, he did not seem to have any plan for pulling the country out of the domestic and foreign impasses of inflation, hostages, and Soviet truculence. The stage was set for a president who would offer a way out and up. It was certain that Reagan's gospel of hope would find receptive audiences. American politics had been in the doldrums since Watergate, and the memory of the defeat in Vietnam still rankled. Goldwater's vision of a southern and western strategy to build a new Republican majority, with which Nixon might have succeeded except for Watergate, was broadened by Reagan to include religious evangelicals with their teleministries, new conservative intellectuals with fertile ideas, and disaffected blue-collar Democrats, and thereby to exploit the intellectual exhaustion of liberalism.

Exit polls on election day revealed, however, that the voters had rejected Carter more than they had approved Reagan. The new president won only 28 percent of the eligible voters, only half of whom voted. His victory was less a triumph of conservative ideas than a sign of voter discontent.[14] And it set up an interesting puzzle. People liked Reagan, but his policies did not have the support of popular majorities. The national reaction against government was congenial to Reagan's celebration of individual liberty, self-help, and patriotism. But skepticism about government did not necessarily translate into support for conservative programs. However, Reagan had an opportunity to forge a mandate by his actions in office. He had brought a much clearer sense of purpose to the campaign than had Carter, who was the leader of a deeply divided Democratic coalition. He had campaigned on the themes of cutting taxes and budgets and increasing defense spending. The country faced an annual inflation rate of 12 percent, an unemployment rate of over 7 percent, a prime lending rate of 20 percent, and a renewed Cold War. Reagan's public approval rating on assuming office was lower than that of previous modern presidents, but his actions brought those figures up quickly. A Republican Senate had not been expected. Nor had thirty-three new Republicans and southern Democrats in the House been anticipated. But unlike Eisenhower and Nixon, Reagan had run with his party. Many politicians saw Reagan's victory as an important step in a partisan realignment in which the Republicans would become the new majority. Congressional Democrats were reluctant to challenge such a victory or the leader who produced it. This was a bit surprising, since vigorous presidential leadership would be the best way to move toward realignment. But the Democrats in Congress were too stunned and too afraid to mount an offensive against the new president, who in his inaugural address promised "restoration, renewal, optimism."

THE FIRST YEAR

Reagan's early decisions were direct contradictions of Carter's early mistakes. He assembled an experienced White House staff, reached out to members of Congress in private meetings, and devoted his first year to passing his economic and defense programs, while putting foreign policy on the back burner. The strategy was articulated during the transition by a staff memo recommending just such a focus.[15] The overriding spirit of the early weeks was one of optimism and confidence. The State of the Union Message asked for the economic program. This was followed by televised talks to the nation and extensive briefings of congressional Republicans by the White House. The president's support began to rise in the polls to majority numbers. His language depicted the nation as a ship out of control, and the promise of recovery was based on the clear assumption that the key to improvement in the economy was the confidence in the future expressed by the president. The Democrats were demoralized, disorganized, leaderless, and intimidated by the polls.

Reagan did not ask anyone to sacrifice. The rate of government spending, but not the absolute amount, would be reduced. The "safety-net" programs for the poor would be protected. The effect of his plans would be the liberation of the economy for the benefit of all.[16] Such confidence was based on the new theory of supply-side economics, which had penetrated the Reagan campaign and become gospel by the time of the inauguration. The theory claimed that investment in the economy was constrained by high taxes and that tax cuts tilted toward potential investors would more than make up any deficit by a surge of economic growth. The theory was plausible and accepted in principle by many economists, but the hard questions were empirical. How much tax reduction would produce what yield in economic activity? The theory was attractive to Republican politicians who hoped to break out of the party's budget-balancing doctrine, which had often resulted in recessions and election defeats. Two Republican members of Congress, Jack Kemp and David Stockman, had written a memo to the president-elect advising him to declare a state of emergency in the economy that would require the implementation of drastic measures: tax and budget cuts. Stockman had been appointed director of the Office of Management and Budget on inauguration day, and he went to work on the revised budget for fiscal year 1992. Supply-side theory was inconsistent with Reagan's economic ideas, which had deplored deficits, but it was certainly consistent with an economics of hope. It was as much political strategy as economic theory because it promised to spread prosperity to all classes without any pain. Nor were the budget cuts prepared by Stockman very radical. They were much less than the proposed tax cuts.

There was a problem, however. It did not take Stockman long to realize that if defense spending was to be increased substantially, and Medicare and Social Security were not to be cut, the projections of federal deficits in future years were bleak. It was necessary for him to create a category of unspecified budget cuts in the near future. Stockman had originally hoped for far greater budget cuts than became politically feasible, and, as the Democrats began to add tax-cutting items to please their constituents, he proposed to the president that tax cuts be delayed in return for agreement with Congress on additional spending cuts, especially in Medicare, Social Security, and veterans' benefits.

These three entitlements cost more than half the domestic budget. Reagan would not hear of it. This would be admitting that the supply-siders had been wrong in their claims for economic policy. He had promised to cut taxes, and he would do so. Stockman did not feel that Reagan understood the economic analysis. But Stockman may have failed to comprehend Reagan's political analysis. The president must do what he had promised to do and must not falter or the game would be lost. Nor was Reagan about to cut entitlements.[17] It was unrealistic of Stockman to fault Reagan for not seeking more drastic spending cuts when his political advisers had made it clear that it was not possible. In addition, Reagan had become a true believer in the supply-side theory and saw no contradictions in its claims. He ignored the debate between traditionalists and supply-siders in his circle.

None of the senior White House staff, including Chief of Staff James Baker, realized at the time how much the deficits would multiply without more severe spending cuts. Their eyes were on the importance of early legislative success. There were critical voices among friends. Murray Weidenbaum, the chair of the Council of Economic Advisers, derided Stockman's initial economic forecast as "fantasy" and forced some change. Republican senators, expert in economic policy, warned the president of future deficits. But he had a doctrine, and a complementary political strategy, and paid no heed. The president had always learned from personal experience and was not open to academic arguments. Baker later acknowledged that he had let the debate get away from him, and wished that he had listened to the Senate Republicans.

To his credit, Reagan practiced no deceit in his rhetorical support for the economic program. He believed in it. However, there was opposition in Congress. The situation was transformed in March by the attempt on the president's life and the gallantry with which he was seen by the public to face it: "I forgot to duck." The event seemed to give him larger-than-life qualities. After his return to active duty, he spoke to Congress in person in April, and then again in July, endorsing a grand compromise of Republicans and southern Democrats. The Economic Recovery Act was passed in August.[18]

What did Reagan personally contribute to the legislative achievement of 1981? The political context was favorable to success. Presidents who have partisan control of Congress, with strong party support for their programs, and who appear to the public to be addressing important national problems in a constructive way are likely to get their programs passed. Reagan's contributions were several. He refused to dilute his program and presented that appeal to the public. His agenda was small, and he did not ask for much or call for sacrifices. He cast his program as the symbol of hope for the future. And he was lucky, not to be shot, but to have survived with gallantry. It seems unlikely that any other Republican president at that time would have been so effective. Success was due to the combination of a congenial context and Reagan's greatest talents.

But was too high a price paid in the form of subsequent budget deficits and a politics of stalemate between the two parties over taxes and spending until 1993? The president's seeming disinterest in hard economic analysis was perhaps a political virtue with a corresponding fault. But we must admit that a more cautious economic program along traditional Republican lines might have prevented the dramatic manner in which Reagan seized and kept the initiative over the policy agenda for many years to come.

❖ ❖ ❖

DOMESTIC POLICY AND POLITICS

The supply-side economic theorists in the administration had thought it possible to avoid the inflation that would come from taxing less and spending more on defense through the actions of the Federal Reserve Board to keep a lid on the economy even as recovery slowly emerged. This may or may not have been a realistic thesis, but it is not what happened. Instead, the Federal Reserve Board, chaired by Paul Volker, a Carter appointee, so tightened the economy, from fear of inflation, that the country was thrown into a severe recession in 1981 and 1982. The economy did begin to recover in 1983, with inflation much reduced, but there was a human cost. The gross national product fell by $600 million. The average family lost $3,000 in income each year. And the lower half of society absorbed four to five times as much of the economic losses, especially in unemployment, as the upper half.[19] By mid-1982, the unemployment rate was 11.8 percent, the highest since the 1930s. The federal budget deficit in 1982 was $111 billion, and the deficits averaged $200 billion annually from 1983 to 1985. Reagan's public approval rating fell sharply to a low of 35 percent in January 1983, and the Democrats gained twenty-four new seats in the House in the 1982 midterm elections.

The president blamed the recession on the Democrats' spending policies, which he said had caused the high inflation from which the economy had faltered. He insisted that he would stay the course through to economic recovery despite political setbacks. He attacked Democrats in Congress for wanting to rescind the third year of the 1981 tax cut. However, he did agree in May 1982 to a package of tax increases, although not income taxes, and spending cuts designed to reduce the deficit in future years. He reconciled this concession in his own mind by claiming that the tax increases were really tax reforms. Reagan met often with Volker and never challenged the actions of the Federal Reserve Board. The men shared a hostility to inflation. Volker probably saved Reagan's presidency in two ways. First, he implemented policies that markedly cut inflation, and then set the path for economic recovery. It was also helpful that world oil and food prices dropped sharply in those years. Volker's second contribution to the president's political success was the gradual expansion of the money supply by the Federal Reserve Board, beginning in 1982, accompanied by the lowering of discount rates. The economy rebounded in 1983 and 1984, which began the long period of economic recovery for which Reagan took credit in the name of supply-side economics.[20]

Reagan believed that recovery was the result of his having preached the gospel of optimism as he stayed the course through the recession. He had put his confidence on the line to be challenged by events and had won the gamble.[21] He described recovery as an American economic miracle that had broken the Democratic policies of tax and spend. The American people had persevered with the president as cheerleader. He stood with the people against the government. If the recession had continued into 1984, one wonders if Reagan could have been reelected. But his credibility was strengthened by the economic recovery. He had earned new political capital. He was unable to exploit it, though, because he and his two successors were prisoners of the ballooning annual budget deficits of over 200 billion. As the national debt tripled, the president and Congress, as two opposing partisan camps, could not agree on what should be done. There was disagreement about which programs to cut or whether to cut at all, and the indecision was exacerbated by the unpopularity of tax increases. But no set of politicians was courageous enough to address the need to rationalize future spending plans on Social Security and Medicare, and this failure was the driving force behind the deficits. The president was not about to threaten his own approval rating, and congressional leaders, of both parties, would not act without him. Reagan simply would not agree to tax increases; in fact, he never submitted a balanced budget to Congress.[22] Voters are rational in that they make political choices in terms of their knowledge. The budget deficits were invisible to the public for the time being because they had no negative impact on people's lives.

The administration achieved only modest legislative successes in the remainder of the first term. But Reagan had articulated and dictated the political agenda for the present and near future and had placed the Democrats, as the party of spending and inflation, on the defensive. Neither the president nor his staff had deliberately engineered the creation of deficits in order to place Democrats in a trap, but the deficits had that effect. After Walter Mondale promised, in his acceptance of the Democratic presidential nomination in 1984, to raise taxes to reduce the deficit and lost the election so badly, Democrats were unwilling to offer that solution again.

Reagan would have liked to have presided over a partisan realignment comparable to that achieved by Franklin Roosevelt. But it was not possible. Roosevelt had created a new coalition in an act of repudiation of a failed Republican regime. Reagan created only a standoff in which neither partisan camp could gain an enduring advantage over the other. A realignment could come only through the resolution of deficit politics in one direction or another. But the president had not led his cause boldly. His actions fell short of his rhetoric.[23]

Thus, although Reagan was easily reelected in 1984, he was not in a position to ask for a mandate for new policies because the economic promises of his first term were unfulfilled. The deficits were growing larger each year.[24] Public approval of the president remained high during most of his second term, but it was accompanied by stalemate between president and Congress over what to do about deficits. Clearly each set of partisan politicians had political goals that were more important than the reduction of deficits. The budget stalemates expressed the divided sentiments of many Americans who wanted low taxes without reduced benefits from government. As a result, political rhetoric was often divorced from policy action. What Reagan could not achieve politically, he sought rhetorically. For example, his State of the Union Message in 1988 depicted his economic policies as comparable to the writing of the Constitution and the Gettysburg Address.[25]

The major legislation of Reagan's second term was the tax reform of 1986, which succeeded because the way had been paved by congressional entrepreneurs of both parties. There did not seem to be great popular support for such action, but the reforms may have been too complex to be understood. This gave the politicians room to bargain and develop a working coalition. Certainly, Reagan left the White House in 1989 in the midst of a surging economy. But had his promises been kept? The supply-side promise was not achieved. Tax incentives did not spur personal savings, which averaged 5.4 percent of net income in the 1980s compared with 8 percent in the 1970s. The national debt tripled, and interest payments on the debt took a larger percentage of the federal budget each year. The United States became a debtor nation, as deficits were financed in large part by investors from abroad.

The incomes of the well-to-do increased during the decade, and those of the poor declined. Programs for the poor were cut back to a much greater extent than were universal entitlement programs. Inflation was beaten back, however and millions of new jobs were created. It was clear by 1989 that politics had not found a way to give the public government benefits at a cost the public was willing to pay. The politics of pleasure was more popular than the politics of pain.[26]

❖ ❖ ❖

WINDING DOWN THE COLD WAR

Reagan's signal achievement in foreign policy was in working with Mikhail Gorbachev for the reduction of both the arms race and the dangerous rivalry between the two superpowers. It was only when Gorbachev became the Soviet leader in 1984, following a succession of caretaker governments, that new possibilities were opened. Reagan surely would have maintained his initial confrontational mode had Gorbachev not appeared. He permitted himself to be influenced by Gorbachev, but it was more than a matter of personality. Gorbachev appealed to Reagan's long-standing belief that the Cold War could be ended once the Soviets realized that they could not solve their economic problems unless the arms race was wound down. Reagan's insistence in 1981 on an American arms buildup, much of it wasteful and indiscriminate, was designed to put intolerable economic pressures on the Soviets. But his imagination went further than the conventional idea of limited, incremental arms-reduction agreements. He wanted to eliminate nuclear weapons altogether. His strategy was similar to his approach on economic recovery. He would set a goal and stick with it despite intervening ups and downs in its achievement. One acted on faith. There was a strong element of hopeful intuition in this strategy of leadership. As an actor, Reagan had always believed in his own star. He felt that his mother had had psychic powers and felt that he had inherited some of it. Perhaps actors must have faith in a persistent inner voice that tells them that opportunities will come at the right time. Luck and opportunity converge. Reagan brought this sense of personal destiny to politics.[27] He was not insecure, but a man with a relaxed faith that all would come right in the end.

Of course, circumstances do not come right without some nudging, and Reagan could be a pragmatic nudger, despite rhetorical excess like his description of the Soviet Union as an "evil empire" in 1981. He was assisted by the convergence of a number of factors. His wife, mindful of his place in history, encouraged him to be accommodating toward the Soviets, particularly as opinion polls in 1984 revealed public concern that he was too strident and militant. Secretary of State George Shultz was also an important influence in his ability to teach Reagan how his hopes for arms reduction might be concretely realized and to teach Gorbachev the rudiments of market economics toward which the Soviet Union might move as it reduced the heavy load of armaments.[28]

But the master stroke was provided by the president himself in the form of the Strategic Defense Initiative (SDI). It was the foreign-policy counterpart of supply-side economics, and it drew the same ridicule from knowledgeable people. And yet, even more than supply-side economics, it worked, not as a weapon, but as an instrument of foreign policy. Reagan's idea of a shield of nuclear weapons in space that would provide an absolute defense against Russian missiles was a science-fiction fantasy. And yet it reflected the hard-headed belief that the effort to keep up with SDI would break the Soviet bank. There is no question that SDI frightened the Soviet leaders and made them more amenable to arms control.[29] By the same token, Reagan was able to push American policy beyond the conventional doctrine of an arms-race stalemate as providing a guarantee of peace. He did not agree and wanted to end the arms race entirely. It is difficult to separate Reagan the fantasist from Reagan the strategist, and, indeed, they went together. His national security adviser, Robert McFarland, thought that Reagan saw himself as a lone, romantic figure who would save the world from the biblical Armageddon, an idea that had long fascinated him.

The president announced his plans for SDI without asking for a detailed analysis of its feasibility by his military advisers. He perhaps never appreciated the scientific criticisms of SDI any more than he understood the criticisms of supply-side theory. But such criticism may miss the point. Reagan valued such bold ideas as resources for leadership. Details about feasibility did not matter because Americans could set their economy right and win the Cold War because they were Americans. The president's job was to preach hope so that it would become a self-fulfilling prophecy. The details did not matter any more than the literal truth of his many stories and anecdotes mattered. It was the meaning that was important.

Reagan had no idea how to implement his vision of the elimination of nuclear arms. His advisers were distressed when he insisted in a meeting with Gorbachev at Reykjavik, Iceland, in 1986 that all nuclear weapons should be eliminated. This was a contradiction of the long-standing idea of NATO as a nuclear deterrent to the Soviet invasion of Western Europe. The American allies were alarmed. Gorbachev made the demise of SDI a condition, which Reagan refused. However, these two unconventional leaders were way ahead of their advisers in imaginative leaps. And each man seemed to see that possibility in the other. Ever since their first meeting in Geneva in 1985, they had come to see each other as human beings, rather than stereotyped caricatures.[30] No one would deny Reagan the credit for the arms agreements that were eventually negotiated or for his willingness to change his mind about the Soviets. He was able to be flexible because historical events, which he helped bring about, matched his initial aspirations.

❖ ❖ ❖

CENTRAL AMERICA

The struggle between Reagan and the Sandinistas in Nicaragua was a lesson in the inability of the president to connect a policy aspiration with practical plans for its implementation. Someone else had to do that for him, and in this case not only did it happen, but it misfired badly and hurt the president. The Sandinista government had overthrown a brutal dicatorship and taken power just before Reagan became president. By that time, the new regime had made clear its Marxist beliefs and seemed to be on the way toward becoming another Cuba, a gnat to worry the United States in its own backyard. The greatest concern in Washington was that the Sandinistas were providing secret military help to radical insurgents in the civil war in El Salvador. The Reagan administration gradually found itself providing military aid to a group of Nicaraguan exiles, the Contras, who hoped to overthrow the Sandinista regime. The initial idea in Washington was to pressure the Sandinistas to stop their aid to the rebels in El Salvador. There was no thought of overthrowing the Sandinistas. However, Reagan's inattention to the concrete aspects of this plan permitted a bureaucratic war within the administration between pragmatists and zealots, with the latter eventually winning control of the key State Department and embassy posts from which to topple the Sandinistas. Shultz stayed aloof, perhaps out of prudence, because Reagan's rhetoric about the Contras as "freedom fighters" who were comparable to America's Founders discouraged him. Reagan and his advisers did understand that the lesson of Vietnam was that no government could send American forces to swamps and jungles without clear public support, and there was no such support for military adventures in Central America. This left covert action as the only avenue. But secrecy brings loss of control at the top. Second- and third-level officials may go into business for themselves. After Congress in 1984 dictated that no aid to the Contras could go through any American "intelligence" agency, which was directed at the CIA, the entire enterprise moved into the National Security Council, with only nominal supervision by the president and no oversight by Secretary of State Shultz or Secretary of Defense Caspar Weinberger. The stage was set for the great fiasco of Reagan's presidency, the Iran–Contra affair.[31]

In the hopes of winning the release of American hostages in Lebanon by terrorists accountable to the Iranian government, Reagan agreed to a plan to sell military weapons to Iran through Israeli conduits. Such action violated American law against giving aid to "terrorist" nations, but the president was permitted by law to sign a waiver that such action was in the nation's interest, which he did. However, Congress was not informed, as it should have been. Shultz and Weinberger argued strongly against such steps, but their arguments were directed to an imprudent policy, whereas the president was intent on winning the release of the hostages. They were talking past each other. As Garry Wills saw, when advising Reagan, "one had to flatter his dream in order to direct it." Shultz could do that successfully in United States–Soviet relations because Reagan's dream coincided with good policy. This was not the case with the sale of weapons to Iran. The two secretaries therefore found it prudent to keep their distance from the plan.

Although Reagan persuaded himself that the purpose of the sale of missiles was to cultivate "moderates" in a future Iranian government, most participants in the decision thought otherwise. The commission appointed by Reagan to look into the matter, after events had blown up in the president's face, concluded that the purpose had been arms for hostages.[32] But Reagan had convinced himself otherwise. Once he had formulated a "story," it became the basis for his interpretation of events.

But then pathos struck. Colonel Oliver North, a third-echelon staff member of the National Security Council, had found a way to divert money paid for the weapons to the Contras. Even worse, John Poindexter, the president's assistant for national security and North's boss, knew of the diversion but did not tell Reagan. He later told Congress that the president needed "deniability" should the facts ever become public. Reagan would have approved of the diversion, he said. This appeared to be a terrible dereliction of responsibility to the president. But think a minute. There is ample testimony that Reagan's advisers were continually frustrated with their inability to get clear directions from the president about what he wanted done. Competing camps vied to appeal to Reagan's prejudices in hopes of getting what seemed to be a nod to act. Poindexter's decision may have been one example of a larger pattern and problem in getting the president to put his visions in concrete terms. Aides guessed what he wanted because they got no direction. His lack of understanding of details was illustrated dramatically in his performance at a disastrous press conference about the sale of weapons to Iran, when he even denied that a third country had been involved, and his later inability to remember the details of the initial decisions. Even as late as a televised speech to the nation in November

1987, Reagan denied that he had sought arms for hostages, despite his admission that the appearance of such a purpose was clear. The polls made very clear that many people did not believe that Reagan was telling the truth about either the sale of arms or the diversion. But his reputation for not being in charge helped him ride out the difficulty.

One could argue that Reagan was not detached at all, but far too deeply involved. If so, the story is still a good illustration of Reagan's failure to understand that he needed expert help in defining and refining his policy choices before he acted. Vision overpowered the possibilities of policy analysis. Reagan lacked the kind of staff that had managed the first legislative year so skillfully or the help that he had from Shultz in dealing with the Russians. His second-term White House staff did not understand that without such expert help, the president could become the prisoner of his own visions.

❖ ❖ ❖

RHETORICAL LEADERSHIP

Was Reagan a good politician because he was a good actor, or was he a good actor because he was a good politician? Or did the two faculties merge in one political personality who was always acting, in both private and public life? This seems most plausible. Great politicians are, of course, great actors. Franklin Roosevelt once told Orsen Welles that they were the two best actors in America. Both Reagan the actor and Reagan the politician were like Jimmy Stewart, who played himself as a crusading senator in *Mr. Smith Goes to Washington*. As Reagan told Lou Cannon about his speeches as candidate for governor: "My actor's instinct simply told me to speak the truth as I saw it and felt it." Cannon adds that "because the role was genuine, or because Reagan believed it to be so, it was thoroughly believable." Reagan, like Stewart in the film, was appealing to the deep strain of "citizen politician" that Americans like. When asked what voters saw in him, Reagan once answered, "I think maybe they see themselves, and that I'm one of them." As one voter put it in 1984: "He really isn't like a Republican. He's more like an American."[33] Reagan thus behaved as a non-actor who did not so much act as share his reactions to events with others. This helps to explain his skill at persuading people that he was not an extremist. He was too much one of us.

Skilled performers learn to read an audience as they act and to draw feeling from that audience that reinforces their acting verve. Reagan was skillful in this way, from years of experience. He wore a contact lens in one eye to watch the audience and used the other eye, without a lens, to read the text.[34] His background as both actor and company spokesman taught Reagan which themes would win support from audiences all across the country. His ability to strike such chords with ordinary people may help explain why they responded favorably to his ideas, even when they did not necessarily support many of his particular policies. This talent may have dissuaded other politicans from challenging him. Certainly Reagan worked at his craft. His aides said that he was his own best speechwriter, continually working on his speeches, whether to large or small audiences. He was criticized for reading from cue cards in meetings, the assumption being that he was too ill-informed to do more than read from notes written by assistants. This seems less likely when one knows that he constantly worked on such cards in order to be prepared to speak in any meeting that was important to him.

Reagan used television as skillfully as Roosevelt had used radio to speak to large, unseen audiences as though they were individuals or small groups, which for the most part they were. Both men thought of individuals who might be listening as they spoke. But they also had the ability to transcend particular audiences and diverse interests and appeal to values shared by millions of Americans. Reagan recognized this talent in FDR and acknowledged his ambition to inaugurate a new political era, as Roosevelt had done. His first inaugural address was a marvellous symbolic ceremony in which the president, having moved the event from the customary east front of the Capitol to the west, could reach out toward the Washington Monument and the Jefferson and Lincoln memorials and invoke these great presidents, on whose shoulders he wished to stand. This was not superficial symbolism, or it would have fallen flat. He was determined to affirm the greatness and glory of America, not only in the past but for the future.

❖ ❖ ❖

CULTURAL LEADERSHIP

James MacGregor Burns defined moral leadership as the creation of a collective moral purpose shared by both leaders and followers. The words of the leader resonate with the needs, values, and beliefs of the followers. Reagan understood and practiced this kind of leadership.[35] Believability and truth are not necessarily the same. Both leaders and followers may be mistaken, in part or in whole. A demagogue deliberately manipulates beliefs and feelings in followers and distorts reality. But Reagan was not a demagogue. He believed what he said. The validity of what he said is another matter. Polls taken during the 1984 election campaign reveal that many people saw Reagan as a "leader" apart from his positions on particular issues. He believed that his leadership derived from what he said rather than how he said it. He had constructed from his personal experience a cluster of ideas that, while drawn from American traditions, were well matched for the politics of the 1980s. Franklin Roosevelt and Lyndon Johnson spoke and worked within the context of American progressive ideas. The purpose of government was to act to redress injustices in the private sector in order to create new opportunities for individuals to live fuller lives, to which all Americans have a birthright. These ideas sustained progressives from Theodore Roosevelt to Lyndon Johnson, and then their appeal simply stopped. Government seemed less benevolent and more malevolent as it waged an unpopular war, acted on behalf of minorities at the seeming expense of majorities, and engaged in top-heavy and frustrating experiments at social change. There was an ideological vacuum to be filled, and Reagan had an ideology for that purpose.

In Reagan's vision, the new task of government was to free private energies for both economic progress and community. Entrepreneurs had a moral mission to create a good life for all. Citizens had a moral responsibility to look after one another in community endeavors. Individualism was compatible with a community of families, households, and neighborhoods. All of this was in opposition to the self-expressive individualism of "liberalism," which denied the truth that social cohesion relied on adherence to basic truths of morality and religion. America was thus said to be sustained by a civil religion, a divinely given opportunity to bring freedom to all that was as fresh and vital today as when it was articulated by the Puritans of colonial Massachusetts. This individualism within moral community was an authentic expression of a "populist" reaction against liberal elites who had forgotten these fundamental truths and relied on government to do things for people that they could perhaps better do for themselves.

In every one of these tenets, Reagan could stand with the people against government, in favor of freedom and morality, against discredited elites who had served the nation badly. He filled a moral vacuum with a moral message. There was a supporting coalition of groups to which this was a friendly message: economic individualists, religious evangelicals, working people who felt abandoned by their former leaders. But Reagan's message deliberately transcended group appeals and offered to give citizens a coherent interpretation of their society at that time. Citizens need such interpretations as much as they require representation for their particular interests.

This kind of rhetorical leadership met the expectations of Americans about what a president should be about. Reagan played the role beautifully, even though he never completely mastered the job. Many critics of Reagan's rhetorical leadership saw a cheapening of public discourse in which symbol replaced substance and the short-run political benefit prevailed over the long-run necessity. He was taken to task for separating words from deeds and for failing to educate with words because his formulations were far too simple. The constant repeating of false claims as a device to overcome real obstacles, such as economic recovery, in the end distorted the truth. Too much of Reagan's rhetoric was said by critics to have blocked realistic solutions because his successors dared not depart from the supposed truths he had spoken. George Bush's promise on his nomination in 1988 of "no new taxes" was a good example.[36]

These criticisms lack merit if all they call to task is the simplification of messages so that they could be understood by ordinary people. All politicians must do this if they wish to be heard. It is possible to simplify reality, as a guide to action, without distorting it. Reagan's great flaw as a political leader was not that he simplified, but that he did not take the trouble to verify whether he was preaching the truth. He had no respect for reasonable and plausible evidence, even granted that such evidence is always incomplete. All politicians must rely on their intuitive skills because facts will take them only to the point where intuitive leaps must be taken. But Reagan too often leaped without asking. He relied on his personal experience, as all good politicians must because that is the source of their persuasiveness. But they have a corresponding responsibility to make sure that they know what they are talking about. Reagan did not always accept that responsibility.

What are we to make of this president, who was so talented and politically successful, but who seemed lacking in what we expect of a statesman? The journalistic and popular stereotypes of Reagan as unintelligent, poorly informed, detached from government, and rigidly doctrinal are too extreme. Such a politician could never have been elected or reelected, or have enjoyed major policy achievements. In fact, his talent was important for his success, in both domestic and foreign policy. He was able to create a popular politics that sustained his leadership for eight years. Yet much was lacking. Ultimately, he disappoints us, despite our admiration. Perhaps a balanced assessment can be found if we look at his intelligence, his executive style, and the relation between his rhetoric and the actual achievements of his presidency.

❖ ❖ ❖

INTELLIGENCE

Some of Reagan's lieutenants thought him to be intellectually weak and lazy. Congressional leaders often had the same impression. In policy discussions, he told stories and did not even seem to listen at times. Lou Cannon interviewed Reagan more than forty times over a twenty-year period and watched him in many formal and informal settings. He did not believe that Reagan was unintelligent, but he could not understand how his mind worked until he discovered psychologist Howard Gardner's theory of multiple intelligences.[37]

From Gardner's perspective, Reagan had little logical or mathematical intelligence, but was gifted with interpersonal intelligence, by which he could read people and their actions well and adjust his actions accordingly. His ability to act and speak in order to appeal to others served this interpersonal intelligence. His kind of mind made sense of the world through narratives and stories that were not necessarily logical. Stuart Spencer, Reagan's longtime political adviser, agreed with this description, as did Martin Anderson, an economist and policy analyst who served on the White House staff. Richard Wirthlin, Reagan's pollster, who had an academic background, thought Reagan to be "extremely gifted and bright" in briefings on the three or four issues that he took as his own, and Cannon was repeatedly told the same by Reagan's assistants. Reagan stumbled when he had to work from briefing papers in discussions or debates. He tried hard to present the material, as presented to him, as though it were a script. But he often got it wrong because the material had not been worked through his personal experience. He had to understand policy discussions in his own terms because he was bent on explaining the programs to the public; that was his role. Unfortunately, he made no effort to master the material in any subjects except the few in which he was interested, and even his understanding of them was limited.

❖ ❖ ❖

EXECUTIVE STYLE

On the surface, Reagan's administrative practices conformed to the tenets of good management. He delegated easily, saving the big problems for his personal attention. He liked collegial discussions among his associates, but could distance himself from competing claims in order to make up his own mind. But the flaw was his failure to demand better analysis of his choices than he usually got. Anderson complained that the president "made no demands and gave almost no instructions."[38] Senior aides shared the frustration of not being able to discuss issues in any depth with him. His best advisers sought to protect him from his own "credulity" by ensuring that he received contesting arguments before decisions were made. But if well briefed, he could make well-balanced decisions. He hated personal confrontation and wanted his advisers to come to him only when they were in agreement. And yet, he knew his own mind. Anderson thought him to be a "warmly ruthless" man who could not be moved from his basic commitments.

GAP BETWEEN WORDS AND DEEDS

How did Reagan test reality to achieve a balance of rhetorical goals and concrete policies? Or did he try at all? His sense of long-term strategy in regard to economic recovery and eventual rapprochement with the Soviet Union worked well for him and for the country. He was way ahead of his own advisers in this discernment. But he was completely blind to the theoretical fallacies and practical failures of supply-side economic policy and to the great harm done by it to many Americans. He never assumed responsibility for the federal deficit, for which he shared much responsibility. He persisted in a futile policy in Central America that came close to destroying his presidency. In too many cases, his vision failed to provide guidance for policy. He was better at public leadership than he was as the executive head of government. But even as a national leader, he ultimately was deficient because his vision of the limited role of government in the American polity could not be sustained by future demands on government. He thought the Constitution to be a static document in which it was possible to establish a perfect and permanent balance among levels of government, to which judges would adhere without interpretation and within which citizens would solve most of their collective problems with minimal help from government. He left his successors the problem of finding new courses of action for problems that he failed to address, such as the budget deficit and entitlement reform. In the final analysis, he practiced a leadership of "words that succeed and policies that fail."[39]

7

Leadership of the Polity

❖ ❖ ❖ ❖ ❖ ❖ ❖ ❖ ❖ ❖ ❖ ❖ ❖ ❖

The preceding three chapters are organized in terms of the model of leadership set out in Chapter 2. My purpose has been to bring the model to life by asking if the normative and empirical ideas that inspired it have merit. Is skill enhanced by context? Is persuasion more effective than control and, if so, under what conditions? Is discernment the master skill, and how does one verify its presence? Is character a skill? What does cultural leadership entail, and how is it expressed? Can one speak with clarity about teaching reality and the conditions under which it succeeds and fails? We will address these questions carefully, with the sketches that follow as our point of departure.

❖ ❖ ❖

FRANKLIN ROOSEVELT

Franklin Roosevelt's greatest skill was rhetoric. It was most effective in the crisis period of his first term, and then again during World War II. It is possible to be a hero of his stature only in times of great national challenge. He understood compromise and bargaining and knew how to match his legislative goals to those of congressional leaders, particularly in his first term. He relied on persuasion more than control, although the White House regularly employed all the sticks and carrots that influence congressional leaders—from the appointment of judges to the traditional pork barrel. Roosevelt's relations with his cabinet officers and other senior aides relied on inspiration and control more than on persuasion because he did not have to persuade them, particularly since he played them off against one another. There is evidence of his clever use in his first term of heresthetic strategies, such as holding back the repeal of prohibition on beer until Congress had passed bills he wanted. But his greatest failures were heresthetic, especially his effort to pack the Supreme Court. This suggests that heresthetic opportunities are not easily created, and the attempt to do so may seem contrived. They must be potentially present in the structure of the political situation, as with the debates between Lincoln and Douglas.

Roosevelt's great skills served him less well in his second term, not only because of his mistakes, but because the New Deal was at an impasse intellectually and politically. He had hoped for clear, ambitious programs of domestic reform that were intended to improve the lives of the bottom third of Americans. But the New Deal lacked an economic theory about how to get out of the Depression, and the "conservative coalition" closed ranks against additional reform.

His discernment of his strategic tasks as president was acute up to a point. His great strength was flexibility and the willingness to experiment. He had the advantage of Herbert Hoover's rigidity as an example of what not to do as president. He shifted with ease to the political and policy programs of the second New Deal when it became clear that both politics and policy required such a change. He never lost sight of the importance of his hold on the public. Critics have argued that his strategic blind spot was his refusal or inability to give any kind of intellectual coherence to individual programs or the New Deal as a whole. There is plenty of evidence of this failing. But perhaps this was sensible. How could he or anyone else know in advance how untried programs would work, or which of the several purposes would emerge as the most feasible? A president more given to closure might have cut off experiments prematurely or have even failed to cast the net of possibilities wide enough.

Roosevelt's character was a great political asset. He needed attention and dominance, but his narcissism was healthy in its self-confidence. His delight in the seat of power was invigorating to others because he challenged them to do their best. He brought hope to everything he did, and this hope was taken over by the millions of people who supported him. Perhaps he had been underestimated in his earlier career because he had not had the opportunity to preach the gospel of hope to such an extent. Transactional politics does not require it. One might ask about his integrity, for it was often charged that he misled others with false promises. There may be something to this. But he had the difficulties of an empathetic personality. He was open, his antennae were out, he sopped up information, and thus he often gave the appearance that he agreed when he was just trying to charm by listening. Roosevelt could not accommodate all views in the decisions he had to make, and he often tried to straddle opposing positions. This is not the same thing as balancing contradictory policies because of uncertainty about what will work best. It is more of a personal desire to charm everyone and keep all on his side. So he surely misled people. But this failing did not undermine the integrity of his political leadership. The same apparent uncertainties and contradictory stands damaged Jimmy Carter and Bill Clinton. Carter was said not to know his own mind, and Clinton was depicted as a twister. Why was FDR not so charged? I think the answer is twofold. When he was leading bold attacks on problems, he focused all his attention on the main event. His tendency to engage in little duplicities was suppressed. But his manipulations during his second term brought him the same kind of criticism as is directed against his successors. They received no credit for bold leadership because politics required them to struggle in the mine-fields of transactional politics. Roosevelt, unlike Carter and Clinton, also had the advantage of creating a political coalition. It is easier to lead when opportunities for the constituents of one's leadership are expanding. It is much more difficult to lead when political conditions are static and the members of the coalition are fighting among themselves.

Roosevelt certainly provided cultural leadership, and he was quite clear in his own mind about how he was building on the ideas of Jefferson but in twentieth-century conditions. Indeed, the New Deal was, ultimately, an extension of Woodrow Wilson's New Freedom, which was itself an adaptation of Jefferson's credo. Radical policies, such as nationalization of the banks, appealed not at all to Roosevelt. He wished to reform capitalism in order to save it. He always taught in terms of liberal American ideas—for example, justifying Social Security as a form of self-help. He was a powerful preacher of American ideals who taught reality to the public in his expositions of his programs. He talked about what government might do in American society in very concrete terms, explaining events as a way to illustate the reality of situations for people. He could simplify without distortion.

Roosevelt was aware of cultural traps and did his best to work around them. The gingerly way in which he treated American isolationism is clear. Although he was always looking ahead, especially in his leadership during the war and his plans for the postwar period, he was quite willing to take advantage of the politics of the moment, thus promising in the 1940 presidential campaign that American boys would not fight in foreign wars. And his deception about the actual role of the American navy in the North Atlantic in 1941 set a very bad precedent for his successors. He also failed to teach the public about the danger of Japan to American interests, perhaps because he hoped for a diplomatic breakthrough with Japan or because such an effort would have placed his meager teaching on Germany and Europe in jeopardy by suggesting that he wanted war.

Did Roosevelt make a difference in history? One can argue that both domestic reform and war would have come to the United States sooner or later, although this is not a certain conclusion. If a conservative Democrat had been elected in 1932 and had failed to give the nation direction and heart, then reform would have been delayed and perhaps would have taken more radical form. An isolationist president might have kept the United States out of war, at least until the

eventual defeat of Britain. So history would have been different without Roosevelt. He provided the reform leadership that met the expectations of American political culture. This congruence of leaders and
historical moment may cause us to underestimate the importance of
his skill as a reform politician. In my judgment, his greatest legacy to
the American polity was his contribution to the quality of democratic
discourse. His leadership enhanced citizenship.

LYNDON JOHNSON

Lyndon Johnson was a masterful legislative leader who understood
myriad kinds of bargaining and could make them all work for him. His
strategies depended more on control than persuasion. His standard
approach was to find ways to buy off each participant in the bargain.
Even the Great Society was a national bargain, with every social group
and class getting something. All would benefit, and none would lose.
Johnson explained the poor to the well-off in such terms. The goal was
to even the race of life for those who were behind without impeding
the progress of those in the lead. He was underrated as a rhetorical
leader because his personality was ill-suited for television and most of
his set speeches were delivered in a dull manner. But as a preacher, he
could be superb. His speech to Congress on behalf of the voting rights
bill is one example; an even better one is his barnstorming the country
and asking citizens to support action against poverty in order to "do
something you can be proud of." This raw power both bemused and
awed the public, who saw a president who knew how to lead. There is
little evidence of his use of heresthetic tactics. One glaring exception
was the Gulf of Tonkin Resolution, which was primarily an electoral
strategy in the 1964 campaign to affirm his toughness on Communism
and thus steal Barry Goldwater's thunder. He was more controller than
persuader, and his tone with his critics, either in Washington or in the
country at large, was to always ask why they did not acknowledge
what he had done for them and the country. He was a consensus leader

who wanted 100 percent support, but without great deliberation. He controlled his executive lieutenants with a combination of inspiration and intimidation. They put up with the intimidation because of the inspiration and the purposes it served. He was discerning about the opportunities for government reform, both in 1964 in the wake of Kennedy's death and following his victory in the 1964 election. In particular, he probably saw more clearly than any other American politician what could be achieved on civil rights.

Johnson's character was a problem. His determination to dominate simply overwhelmed people. He cajoled and bullied until he got his way. But he was emotionally insecure, and it took many forms: browbeating assistants, attempting to manipulate reporters, dismissing his critics as lacking backbone, lamenting that he was not loved. Once public opinion began to turn against him, he grew defensive and retreated from critics. His insecurity about being a raw Texan with an inadequate education made him too deferential to his well-educated advisers and defensive against criticism from the universities. He could never fully overcome the image of a Texas wheeler-dealer with the general public, and, of course, it had some truth in it.

Johnson was a classic transactional politician as majority leader of the Senate. And he tried very hard to transcend transactional politics when he became president. But the Great Society was a collection of bargains, and his perception of politics as bargaining made it difficult for him to understand why the domestic beneficiaries of his programs should turn against him. He personalized the situation. He did not seem to understand that the North Vietnamese leaders were not bargainers like union leaders and businessmen, whom he had successfully pushed into agreements. Even his management of foreign-policy making was permeated by the craft of the Senate leader who wants everyone on board; he sought consensus more than deliberation as the government lurched further and further into a commitment to South Vietnam.

But the Great Society also embodied a strong, moral vision of a better America, and it would not be fair to say that Johnson did not communicate this vision or convince most people of its value. The programs, despite some evisceration, have continued to the present day and will not be repealed. He taught the American progressive ethic of helping people to help themselves. His experience during the New Deal years inspired the Great Society, which he thought of as an extension of Roosevelt's reforms. Roosevelt was his model for presidential leadership. But he wanted to surpass FDR, who was rival as well as exemplar. Johnson aimed to win a bigger election victory than Roosevelt and pass more legislation. And he was going to do it without repeating FDR's mistakes in attacking the Supreme Court, fellow Democrats, and business leaders. He also practiced Roosevelt's deceits almost to the letter, promising during the 1964 campaign that American boys would not fight in Asia, and manipulating the Gulf of Tonkin incident, much as FDR had manipulated information about the *Greer*.

In the Senate, Johnson was bound by the rules imposed by ninety-five other senators and had to work as a transactional leader. In the White House, he seemed to understand his choices with the same prudence. But he was too filled with vainglory to moderate his pace or loosen his control. He was very good at teaching reality when he spoke from conviction, particularly on civil rights. His words had an authenticity, not only about his own feelings but about the best feelings of the country, and this authenticity was acknowledged by constructive action. But his teaching and preaching about Vietnam lacked conviction because the country had ceased to believe in the message. Americans would acknowledge their collective responsibilities about civil rights. But the Cold War themes were not convincing as the Vietnam War dragged on, without any end in sight. People might have been happy to win and withdraw without a moral qualm. But America's inability to win the war undermined the Cold War justifications that Johnson and his advisers preached. The main cause of the credibility gap that eventually brought Johnson down was his message. His public persona, which became less and less attractive to people, simply made it easier for people to reject him.

Did Johnson make a difference? I would say much less than Roosevelt. The Great Society was an enlargement of Kennedy's New Frontier program, and would have been enacted to some degree with a

Democratic president in the 1960s. The Vietnam War was a cultural trap that a consensus leader could not avoid; it is difficult to imagine any politician finding a politically acceptable way to avoid entanglement. Johnson's contribution to both domestic and foreign policy was intensity. More domestic legislation was passed than would otherwise have been, but with greater prudence the design and implementation of programs might have been more careful. And the war was conducted with more emotional intensity from the White House than perhaps was necessary. A president with greater prudence and sense of irony in history than Johnson possessed might have seen the error more quickly. Johnson would not have been nominated for president in 1968 had Kennedy lived. He was perhaps not the kind of man who should be president. But, having said all that, he must be credited with a creativity in the politics of civil rights that would have eluded any number of presidents. He may have recognized this as his enduring legacy because it was the subject of the last speech of his life, delivered in Austin at the LBJ School of Public Affairs. According to all accounts, it was inspiring.

❖ ❖ ❖

RONALD REAGAN

Ronald Reagan's primary political skill was rhetorical, and he knew how to use it for the best strategic effect. He joined his ability to speak with clever political strategy—campaigning for governor of California, attacking a discredited Jimmy Carter in 1980, seizing a mandate for policy from a demoralized Congress in 1981, persevering with his economic agenda through the recession and on to reelection in 1984, and supplying both force and persuasion in his dealings with Mikhail Gorbachev. He knew how to bargain and was willing to do so, as long as he was able to adhere to his larger strategic vision. He saw himself as a persuader; certainly, he was not a controller. He did seem to rely on heresthetic strategies, in deficit politics with the Democrats and in SDI politics with the Soviet leaders.

Reagan's character was a source of political credibility. His own buoyancy was contagious. He was emotionally self-confident without being arrogant; indeed, his humility seemed genuine, and ordinary people found it appealing. But he often denied facts that did not fit his optimism, such as the ballooning budget deficit. His moral commitments were genuine, but limited in their range. And while no one ever questioned his personal integrity, his actions showed a contempt for government that permitted many of his subordinates to violate not only the ethics of public office, but the written and unwritten rules of respect for the Constitution. Reagan may not have been fully knowledgeable about the details of the Iran–Contra affair, but his cavalier disregard for the law and the wishes of Congress contributed greatly to the mishap that became a scandal. He forfeited his greatest asset, his credibility, because the public did not believe he was telling the truth. For the president to plead ignorance of what his closest assistants were doing is not a contribution to the art of government.

He certainly was a cultural leader; indeed, this was his primary purpose. Delegates to the Republican National Convention in 1980 could not believe it when the nominee invoked FDR's inspiring leadership of the nation in 1933 as his exemplar. But Reagan's praise was genuine. He identified with Roosevelt's courage and confidence. He had long admired the first inaugural address and the fireside chats. Roosevelt's radio talks in the 1930s were surely models for Reagan. But he invoked FDR's more conservative ideas as though they exemplified the essential leader. Perhaps more important, he wanted to be the conservative Roosevelt, an inspirational leader for conservative causes. Roosevelt had been the last "great" president, and Reagan would be the next.

His policy preaching in 1980 fashioned an appealing conservative myth for his time. The Carter administration had been unable to control inflation and increase economic productivity, and the culture of welfare was less and less popular. American national morale was at a low after the Vietnam War, Watergate, two oil shocks administered by the oil-producing nations, the taking of hostages in Iran, and the Russian invasion of Afghanistan. Reagan's ideas were plausible in that historical context and appealed to many people for that reason. However, he was a better tribune for the new Republican party of the South and West, which had been growing since 1964, than he was a leader of American opinion at large. There was always a gap between his grandiose rhetoric about the American promise and his advocacy of particular policies and programs, which was often quite vague. So citizens could respond simply to the preaching about America, at a time when it was needed. Most of the White House public relations work focused on getting good photo opportunities and news bites for the president day in and day out. People responded positively. Reagan looked like a leader. But opinion surveys taken over the eight years of Reagan's presidency indicated no widespread conversion to conservative ideals among the American public. Reagan was rewarded politically for his style, his persona, and, most important, the fruits of economic recovery. It is rational for citizens to judge a government by its achievements. Efforts by Walter Mondale and others to make Reagan responsible for the mushrooming federal deficit did not work politically because ordinary people could not be persuaded that the deficit was a problem. The problem was academic; it could not be seen.

Did Reagan teach reality, or was his domestic leadership one grand illusion? He was certainly more preacher than teacher, albeit a very sincere one. He fell far short of what one would expect a president to do as a teacher. His greatest strength as a speaker was on ceremonial occasions: the speech on the fortieth anniversary of D-Day, and the response to the explosion of the *Challenger*. But there was little guide to policy here. He did not do the personal homework to discover if the claims he was making for his policies had validity. He out and out preached illusion in his prescriptions for government. His conception of that government was stuck in the nineteenth century in the vision of separate levels of government doing different things, with the federal government doing the least. He was unwilling to recognize possible future demands on government. And he completely failed to see flaws in his own programs. He knew so little about the actual operations of his administration that senior aides were desperate for guidance. Yet he was seldom challenged for fear that the challenger would lose out to those who claimed to be the guardians of Reagan's deepest wishes. So subordinates often went into business for themselves.

Reagan's leadership was an interesting combination of the adherence to long-term strategies that were often successful and the refusal to buy trouble by proposing policies that might be unpopular in the short run. Thus deficit reduction was avoided if it meant raising taxes, and reforming Social Security was taboo. Reagan had plenty of prudence when it came to protecting himself for the things that were important to him.

Did Reagan make a difference? It is likely that a conservative Republican administration would have been elected sooner rather than later. But Reagan, like Roosevelt, gave it a superb rationale that, again like Roosevelt's presidency, created the new political agenda with which the nation is still working. He made a genuine contribution to the end of the Cold War, but it was primarily his willingness to take Gorbachev seriously and cooperate with him. Gorbachev made the difference, not Reagan.

Reagan's principal fault as a political leader was his failure to contribute to the improvement of democratic discourse. He bears a heavy responsibility for the crude way in which George Bush was elected president in 1988, with slogans rather than ideas and policies. He was too much the crowd pleaser, the preacher who did not tell uncomfortable truths, the spinner of illusions. His rhetoric had a certain autodidactic quality, as though the president were talking to himself, trying to reassure himself that everything was all right. The appeal to illusion, which characterized his entire life, was his great political strength, but also his greatest weakness as a political leader.

❖ ❖ ❖

COMPARISONS OF THREE PRESIDENTS

The model of leadership emerged in explicit form as I was writing the three presidential profiles. The sentiments and ideas with which I began the study were given explicit form and expression. The ideas of Aristotle were my touchstone at the beginning. I am drawn to Aristotle because I think that he describes the tasks of leadership accurately. He also combines the empirical and the normative in one formulation, and I have tried to do the same here.

Propositions derived from the model may be illustrated by the political careers of Roosevelt, Johnson, and Reagan. Nothing can be proved, but we will have a framework for further analysis.

1. Political abilities—in the form of skillful use of the strategies of bargaining, heresthetics, and rhetoric—are most effective when they are congruent with strong supportive politics in the polity. Skill contributes to the availability of political support, of course, and the interaction between skill and context adds creative elements that cannot be predicted. Each takes strength from the other.

Roosevelt's first term, Johnson's years of legislative achievement, and Reagan's initial command of Congress and creation of a new political agenda—all bear witness to this proposition.

2. Skill alone is not sufficient for legislative achievement when the political tides are moving away from a president. In fact, skills that have been effective may become caricatures and do more harm than good if the political environment that elicited their creativity has vanished.

Roosevelt's skills misfired more often than not in his second term over domestic issues because, in the absence of political support, they appeared to be more manipulative than persuasive. Johnson was increasingly isolated in both domestic and foreign policy as his strategies of control generated backlash that he could not dominate. Reagan's inspirational power was valueless when it was wasted on the defense of his own credibility in the Iran–Contra affair. No one believed him.

3. Discernment of the historical possibilities for action is the master skill that provides guidance for bargaining, heresthetics, and rhetoric. Rhetoric is the chief instrument of strategy because it is used to convey a sense of purpose. Bargaining and heresthetics are instrumental, secondary skills.

Each of these presidents had a good strategy for uniting politics and policy in his presidency. Their strategies gave broad political plausibility to their purposes and were the main source of their public support. But it was inevitable that their very political successes would create opposition with which their kind of politics could not cope. Roosevelt's New Deal finally ran up against the limits set by the political culture. Johnson's Great Society unleashed forces antagonistic to reform. Reagan's disdain for government could not displace its necessity.

4. Persuasion is a more effective instrument of influence than control. This is a difficult proposition to illustrate, since persuasion and control intermingle. One seldom persuades by reason alone. Control in some form—whether based on fear, desire, or more mundane political incentives—usually must be present if persuasion is to be effective. And yet there is no pure form of control without some persuasion.

This proposition should apply not to the details of particular cases, but to an appraisal of an overall career. Roosevelt did plenty of controlling, but he was successful primarily because he could persuade others to follow him. How else do we interpret the aftermath of his first inaugural address? Of course, he persuaded by action as well as words, and action was needed in 1933. But it was persuasion nonetheless because Americans could see serious efforts to help them. Johnson did plenty of persuading in individual cases, particularly with domestic legislation. But the Great Society programs were rammed through Congress without sufficient deliberation, and the entry into Vietnam was forced on the nation in the guise of continuity with past policy. This was deception. But ultimately such control did not work, even though a terrible price was first paid. Reagan was not a controlling leader. But his strategies of persuasion fell far short of real achievement, in the long run, because of their shallowness. Persuasion that is not grounded in the reality of a situation is temporary because it does not address the real problem at hand.

5. Character is both a skill and a political resource. Roosevelt's psychological health radiated confidence and hope. Johnson's insecurities took indirect form in his efforts at control in ways that eventually isolated him from the nation. Reagan's buoyancy was much like

FDR's, and it had the same positive political effects. But he was also a psychological prisoner of illusions.

The moral commitment of these men to the policies they advocated was very important for their success. They reached beyond simple transactional politics to persuade people that what they wanted was the right thing to do, for its own sake. But what about integrity? Was personal integrity necessary to public acceptance of their leadership? I think so because they suffered greatly when their word was doubted, and thus their integrity was questioned.

6. Cultural leadership consists of adapting old ideas to new purposes. It is creative and cannot be predicted. Roosevelt, Johnson, and Reagan were political innovators. The combinations of ideas, values, and political appeals that they concocted did not come from party platforms or the work of intellectuals. Rather, they were the fruits of many years of political experience. But experience is not enough. The kind of creative politician that they embodied is tenacious and ambitious, but ambition alone does not explain the faculty that such men are driven to exercise. It is the need and the desire to explain the world to others, less for enlightenment than as the basis for a political career. Ambition and idealism are thus commingled.

7. When prudence is forgotten, failure is guaranteed. A politician who is guided only by prudence will venture little. A politician who lacks prudence will overreach. Leaders must assess the possible limits to action before they can be bold. The enduring achievements of these presidents were grounded in their prudence. They knew better than to try to do the unthinkable, and when they acted imprudently, they paid a political and personal price.

But is this the advice of a conservative guided by sensitivity to contingency, paradox, irony, and the certainity of ambiguity? And is it consistent with the strong advocacy in this book of leadership as moral agency? The best answer that I can give is to suggest that much American political leadership, whether progressive or conservative, suffers from a lack of awareness of contingency and the uncertainty of action. This is part of the shallowness of the American liberal tradition. To ask idealists to be realistic is not to reject idealism but to ask them to be more effective.

8. To "teach reality" is to teach the spirit of the constitution of a polity, to combine practical reason and moral purpose, and to use such "discernment" to win support for concrete policy ideas.

There is no objective test of "reality," but it is not wholly subjective because it is shared. The teacher of reality succeeds when he provides an analysis of problems in their historical context, and adds to that analysis plausible solutions. Such teaching must respect facts and evidence, but it cannot be proven to be valid. It can only be plausible. There will always be uncertainty as history is interpreted and reinterpreted. But the successful political leader is the one who offers the most plausible interpretation of reality. Citizens want such interpretations as much as they want their particular interests to be served. And they also seek a sense of collective moral purpose, even when they disagree on important moral questions.

Solid achievement cannot be secured by illusions. But the discernment exercised by creative politicians and the prescriptions they offer on the basis of that discernment must necessarily go beyond available knowledge. Plausibility means taking things on faith. Roosevelt was the most plausible politician of our three presidents. Despite his exuberant idealism, he kept in close touch with the concrete aspects of politics, policy, and administration and relied on a great variety of informants. Johnson was very good at developing political intelligence, but he never tested policy proposals against empirical analysis. He used ideas as tools of persuasion and control. Thus it is no wonder that he eventually lost touch with reality. Reagan was even more the victim of illusion. He was very skillful at appealing to moral sentiments, especially on ceremonial occasions. But he almost completely lacked the ability to test his ideas against concrete experience and evidence.

9. Presidents must recognize "cultural traps" and find ways around them, but they are usually too strong to be overcome. It may be possible to invoke a counterprinciple in American political culture.

For example, FDR eventually overcame isolationism with the promise of a role for the United States in aiding the Allies in the defense of freedom. Woodrow Wilson had used the same argument to justify the nation's entry into World War I. The problem was that the crusade to "make the world safe for democracy" itself became a cultural trap of American messianism let loose on the world. It may be very difficult for presidents to realize that they are falling into an implicit cultural trap as they respond to events. Johnson and his advisers discovered this with Vietnam.

10. The question of whether it is politically difficult to "teach reality" in the political short term is a very complex one. There are many examples of failed attempts. This is a reality of democratic politics. However, there are also many instances in which prudent leaders have prepared the public in the short run for long-term possibilities. Roosevelt did this in his effort to prepare the nation for possible war. He used events to teach reality. Success in linking short-term appeals to a long-term objective also depends on events as they unfold, but prudent leaders can be ready.

There is no antidote in this theory for the politician who deliberately uses short-term appeals to prevent the consideration of a long-term problem. Johnson did it in 1965 by avoiding any discussion about the financing of the Vietnam War. Reagan could be said to have done it by deliberately stifling public discussion of the budget deficit. His opponents could not find a politically acceptable way to address deficit reduction until a severe recession during the Bush administration cast Reagan's entire project in doubt. Thus by resorting to short-term maneuvers for reasons of political expediency, politicians may exacerbate problems, thus making them more difficult to solve in the long run.

These propositions, as stated, have a utilitarian flavor. They seem to suggest that presidents will be effective if they follow the maxims. Of course, no such rules can completely guarantee leaders' success in dominating events in the face of the wild cards of politics and government. But even so, a president who exercises discernment intelligently has taken the first step toward effectiveness no matter how difficult the problems to be faced. But there are other hard questions to be answered: Is it always politic to tell the truth or never to lie? Is persuasion really more effective than coercion in an imperfect world? Is it not tempting to appeal to cultural traps to protect oneself from political enemies or to take advantage of them? Leaders must win in politics in order to do good things. These are Machiavelli's questions.

Machiavelli provides his own answers. To the degree that the citizens of a polity are good citizens, leaders will be able to lead according to the norms of the republic. The compromises with morality required in turbulent politics are justified by necessity. But Machiavelli also permits even the leaders of a good republic to be demagogues for the glory and power of the state. I have no hesitation in rejecting that belief. But the question of a sliding scale of morality in relation to degrees of virtue in a republic is more difficult. That leads to considerations of ethics that are beyond this study, even though they are important.

Truth telling and persuasion are better instruments of action in American democracy than lying, control, and demagogy as long as citizens respond to "the better angels of our nature." Leadership based on those two principles has two consequences for the quality of democratic life. It nourishes the practice of truth telling in politics, thus permitting us to potentially confront the real problems that face us. And American democracy must receive infusions of idealistic leadership if it is to be true to the purposes for which the Union was founded. American politics is transactional much of the time, and properly so. Even transactional politics is based on national idealism, or it would deteriorate into a war of all against all. But we must consciously take stock of our national myths and adapt them to new realities and thus reach beyond transactional politics.

I assign these responsibilities to all politicians in our government. Presidents are not the only guardians of national ideals. The beginning of wisdom for presidents is to understand that they share power with Congress, the courts, and the states. But this is all the more reason for presidents to invoke ideals, when appropriate, because ideals are the strongest persuaders. The presidency is a seat of power and an engine for policy making, but it is also a moral agent for the articulation of the ideals of American democracy. The character of American governmental institutions and political culture invites presidents to be moral leaders. This maxim does not apply solely to innovative presidents. Even the most cautious and conservative presidents are called on to invoke principles as a basis for their actions. Creative politics in the presidency is more difficult and more daring because principles must be reinterpreted. But all presidents should be moral leaders.

The rest of this chapter explores the dimensions of the model of political leadership, returning to our three presidents but reaching beyond them to general insights about leadership.

❖ ❖ ❖

SKILL IN CONTEXT

Historical accounts of large political transformations, such as the American and French revolutions, do not explain such upheavals by a "great man" theory of history. Leading men are more often presented as symbols of a larger drama. But this is the lazy way of assessing leadership. What difference may leaders make? One can suggest the historical conditions in which politicians may make a difference. They must have purposes and the ambition to shape events. The historical situation must permit more than one course of action. Their recognition of the key contingencies to be shaped is crucial because so much is not uncertain. The opportunity to reinterpret political goals and incentives must exist, and leaders must seize that opportunity, not to remake the society, but to point it in new directions. There will be a fusion of the new and the old.

Sidney Hook drew a distinction between "eventful" man and "event-making" man.[1] The first has no special qualities, but is able to influence events because of the position he holds. Harry Truman provided leadership in the formation of American policy for the Cold War because he was president, but he was not a uniquely creative leader.

The second kind of leader makes a difference because of his great talent, intelligence, and will. Hook sees Lenin as such a man. The second Russian Revolution would not have occurred without Lenin's seizure of the opportunity. The eventful man is more likely to be the agent of many others, whereas the event-making man directs the actions of followers.

It would seem that, by Hook's definition, the event-making leaders of the twentieth century have been dictators: Lenin, Stalin, Hitler, Mao. What of democratic heroes: the two Roosevelts, Wilson, Churchill, de Gaulle, Nehru, Mandela, even Gorbachev? Hook did not address this question directly, but he would seem to rule them out as event-making leaders because he regards such leadership as incompatible with democracy. Event-making leaders are too ambitious to respect constitutional restraints because of their desire to put their stamp on history.

Hook has drawn the distinction too sharply. It is the same mistake that James MacGregor Burns made with transactional and transforming types. Eventful, transactional politicians are common and easy to spot. Democracy could not thrive without them. But bold and creative leaders who seek political change transcend the transactional style without conforming to the event-making, transforming ideal. They are creative in adapting political culture, but act within the restraints of democratic norms.[2] They do not act alone, and they build on the work of many others, but it is their talent to articulate and lead the way toward a new interpretation of the political culture. The democratic heroes of the twentieth century, including our three presidents, were this type of leader. The primary skill of such leaders is discernment of creative possibilities in a changing historical context. This is not to say that they knew what the results of their action would be. No one can transcend the history within which he or she works. They are most effective as they work through, and yet find ways to transcend, transactional politics.

We therefore conclude that character is of crucial importance. One does not have to be an event-making or a transforming leader to have a positive or a negative impact on the practices of politics. Such practices may be an extension of character.

CHARACTER

Character is a skill. Inner confidence will be contagious. Inner security will permit growth. Weaknesses of character may prevent the sharing of confidence and may impair political learning. Harold Lasswell invented the idea of "political man," who enters politics as a means of overcoming low self-esteem. The need for the approval of audiences, for example, may drive the agitator, and such a need, being unconscious, is insatiable. Action has a driven quality. Lasswell contrasted this type of leader with a "democratic character," who is emotionally confident and open to the thoughts and needs of others in ways that a "political man" can never be.[3] It was Lasswell's hope that democratic polities would promote the citizenship of democratic character so that there would be less scope for insecure politicians. But Lasswell did not say whether politicians with democratic character also have to have a high order of political skills. Character does not guarantee skill. Perhaps democratic character may supplant skill.

James David Barber continued Lasswell's distinction in his depiction of "active positive" and "active negative" politicians.[4] The active positives are energetic and have high self-esteem. They do not carry their insecurities into politics. The active negatives are driven and energetic, but are much less self-confident and self-accepting. They use politics to bolster their self-esteem. But they may act out their insecurities in their political work. We can identify such politicians, but the active-positive category is too broad because Barber, like Lasswell, did not ask if some active positives are more politically skillful than others and whether that makes a difference. If it does, what are the attributes of skillful politicians who are also democratic characters?

The psychiatrist George Vaillant has provided some clues to an answer. He pointed out that all people utilize mechanisms of defense by means of which they balance desire, conscience, relationships with others, and the demands of the external world.[5] They invent ways to manage competing demands. The "mature" defenses are those that permit people to find a unity among such demands that is comfortable and coherent, with a high degree of freedom to adapt to the world. Conversely, the "immature" defenses fail to reconcile conflicts among competing demands.

Roosevelt's political personality was built on mature defenses, whereas Johnson was often at war with himself. Johnson could harness his skills to political tasks, but his uncertainty about himself could cause him to use his skills to a fault so that his desire for control was the enemy of learning. Immature defenses fail to moderate such tensions.[6] Vaillant used the term "ego maturity," much as Lasswell spoke of "democratic character." But his analysis suggests that secure, skillful politicians develop their political skills as one aspect of their mature defenses.

Stanley Renshon, a political scientist and psychoanalyst, has argued that strong personal ambition may be both a creative and a destructive force. He posits the psychological makeup of persons who are secure in their ability to lead in democratic ways and use good judgment as they make decisions.[7] He noted a difference between those who use their ambition in the service of ideals and those whose ideals are employed primarily in the service of ambition.[8] One may infer that the former are Lasswell's democratic characters and the latter are his political men. It seems reasonable to postulate that political skill and democratic character are combined in the mature defenses of the best politicians. They want to lead, and they lead, with skill, from emotional strength. This was certainly true of Roosevelt. His needs and talents reinforced one another and were combined with an acute sense of reality. Johnson's skills and insecurities seem to have fed one another. His exercise of skill never satisfied his insatiable insecurity.

❖ ❖ ❖

CULTURAL LEADERSHIP

In the discussion of skill in context, the term "discernment" is used to mean a broad assessment of the possibilities for policy achievement in a given time. Discernment provides the best guide to the use of bargaining, heresthetics, and rhetoric. I deliberately narrow the term in regard to cultural leadership to mean insight into what can be achieved, in politics and policy, according to the cultural beliefs and values of citizens and their political leaders. Culture provides resources for action and sets limits on what can be achieved. Knowledge of such cultural resources and limits is discernment. This is not book knowledge, but intuition based on experience and the ability to read people in politics. Leaders must know the content of the culture to be able to assess the appropriate balance between purpose and prudence.

Roosevelt had a superior understanding of prudence in comparison with Johnson and Reagan. He never attempted to push the New Deal beyond the bolstering of capitalism, and he was cautious as he introduced new parts of the emerging welfare state—for example, describing Social Security in terms of individuals helping themselves. Johnson understood the pressure of the electoral calendar on the possibility of legislative achievement, but because he defined such achievement as the test of a successful presidency, he did not prepare the old New Deal constituencies of blue-collar workers for the forces unleashed by the civil-rights movement. Perhaps this could not have been done, but he did not try. The War on Poverty program, for example, was rammed through Congress and pushed on localities without sufficient political dialogue or administration foresight.[9] Reagan was more lucky than discerning in his domestic programs. He had been saying the same things for sixteen years and was elected to the presidency only as the Democratic coalition was exhausted. His vision far outran the possibilities for action. He had only one good legislative year. He was never able to persuade public majorities of the need for the revolution in government that he sought. Thus his presidency was more of a standoff than a period of high achievement.

All three presidents worked within the implicit limits of American cultural beliefs. Reform to the left stops when it appears to threaten the autonomy of a large number of citizens. Reform to the right stops when it appears to threaten the opportunity of a large number of citizens. Americans are rhetorical conservatives and pragmatic liberals. Discovery of the correct balance of boldness and prudence for a given time is best guided by an understanding of the cultural possibilities for action and the cultural limits to action.

Critics of American political culture would introduce a strong dose of the principle of community so that economic individualists would acknowledge legitimate restraints on the uses of economic power and social individualists would reach beyond the palliatives of modest social programs. American liberalism, in its two halves, would recognize that the community precedes the individual. It is not my task here to analyze this distinguished body of literature.[10] As things stand now, the resources of American political culture are not as rich as these critics would wish them. I take my text from Seymour Martin Lipset, who has argued that we should forget about trying to reform American ideologies and work within them. He sees the American creed as consisting of liberty, egalitarianism, individualism, populism, and laissez-faire.[11] These beliefs and values have developed through major historical events and are, in this sense, authentic. We quarrel in politics about how to apply the basic principles of "Americanism" on which we agree. The American creed is a two-edged sword in which a high sense of personal responsibility, individual initiative, and voluntarism balances with self-serving behavior and disregard for the common good. Those who call for a new emphasis on communitarian norms do not understand that the American tradition favors "moral individualism" as the correct path to reform. Lipset adds: "The idea that we can be better moral agents by passively soaking up the values of the social context in which we find ourselves is antithetical to the principles of our democratic culture." In America, "individualism strengthens the bonds of civil society rather than weakens them."[12]

Robert Wiebe agrees with Lipset in his conclusion that "popular self-government" in the United States has always contained the culturally specific principle of "individual self-determination."[13] He sees a crisis of governance today because the cultural characteristics that have emancipated individuals who seek personal fulfillment have trapped them in a democracy whose structures of centralized power do not seem responsive to them. Thus Americans have expressed a strong popular desire to romanticize politics by turning to a leader above politics, whether Reagan or Ross Perot. Wiebe rejects the idea of importing alien ideas of community into American politics because those theorists who would do so lack "historical awareness" of how problems have been framed and resolved in the past. The contribution of history is to "find out what fits." The overarching principle of reform that fits is "a reaffirmation of the American heritage that draws people with all kinds of identities and loyalties into a collective self-governing process." In the United States, such reform is inspired by individualism, "either as self-determining or as fulfillment." To single out American individualism as the cause of our collective problems is to fly in the face of our history. Wiebe understands that the sum of "rights" demanded by citizens may grow so large that government is disabled. No one knows when that point would be reached. But he places his confidence in the principle of making sure that the majority of citizens retain control over their government. The democratic process must be broadened. But politics always must recognize the central principle of the American creed: "To act without receiving harm in public and to act without doing harm in private are fundamental to democratic individualism."

In this study, I have discussed pairs of opposites: the politics of self-interest versus the politics of the general welfare; the politics of economic individualism and humanistic individualism, a constitutional presidency versus a leadership presidency, and transactional versus moral and cultural leadership. And yet we have concluded that these opposites merge in practice. Thus both American conservatives and liberals appeal to moral individualism. The political clash of interests and values runs throughout the paired opposites. Transforming leaders must have transactional skills. These divergent and yet overlapping appeals are recognized by citizens as authentic because they accept both elements of each dichotomy. They refuse to choose one or the other but lean in one direction or the other, depending on the contingencies of a given time.[14] Discerning political leaders are able to sense the right balance for a given time and act boldly or prudently, according to what their discernment advises. Thus teaching reality is in large part about affirming the American principles that may be invoked and eliciting an authentic response from the public at different times in history.

❖ ❖ ❖

TEACHING REALITY

It is human nature to seek to understand reality in all its many aspects. We do not fully succeed, but that does not stop us from trying. Even politicians, who work from conventional wisdom, are pushed by their craft to learn new things. If they also choose to propagate illusion, they may know the difference between illusion and reality. Our purpose here is to ask what teaching reality implies for leadership in the American polity. If practice falls short of realistic ideals, then the fault may be in the politicians or in the polity.

I agree with Richard Rorty that human "solidarity" is achieved not by inquiry, but by "imagination."[15] Truth is created as well as found. The Founders of the United States created new political reality when they wrote the Constitution. Abraham Lincoln articulated new truths about the Union at Gettysburg. Individual lives and the histories of polities are "dramatic narratives" that never achieve final form. And the creators of new ideas must rely on the vocabulary of the culture in which they work. We have to start from where we are. The chief instrument of innovation, then, is a talent for "speaking differently, rather than arguing."

Michael Oakeshott has cited Pericles' speech to the Athenians during the Peloponnesian War as ideal political rhetoric.[16] Pericles diagnosed the situation, made a proposal, assessed possible consequences, balanced the merits of the plan against other ideas, and assumed agreement about general goals. Oakeshott sees Pericles as following Aristotle's maxims for rhetoric, in which there is reasoning without the use of axioms and recommendation of action in a contingent situation. The arguments constructed from such rhetoric cannot be logically refuted because the major premises are not stated and the recommendations are based only on possibilities. Such language, for

Aristotle, is based on beliefs generally held to be true and values generally held to be important. Political argument that appeals to abstract ideas must also use concrete referents if the audience is to understand the relevance of the ideas. Claims are persuasive rather than demonstrable. Only probabilities are weighed. This is Aristotle's practical wisdom. The creative politician does not argue from a deductive schema, but draws on his skill, experience, and political knowledge to make arguments. His rhetoric is part of a larger strategy of action guided by discernment.

Aristotle believed that appeals to truth and justice are likely to prevail over their opposites if the speaker is skillful at rhetoric. Truth is easier to prove than falsehood because the underlying facts support it. And since the true and approximately true are apprehended by the same faculty, the leader who makes a good guess at truth is likely to make a good guess at probabilities. The speaker is more likely to succeed at persuasion when he has personal credibility with his audience, making him more believable than others. This is especially the case when certainty is impossible and opinions are divided. Character is the best means of persuasion that a good man possesses.[17]

Aristotle recognized that the understanding of justice is conditioned by the character of the polity. Thus rhetoric, as one form of practical wisdom, would necessarily match the character of politics. In cities with good laws, in which citizens are educated in virtue, a speaker need only prove the facts to be as claimed. In the best polities, all citizens have practical wisdom about politics and the claims of rhetoric. Mismatches between wise politicians and citizens who are not prepared for them will occur, and special rhetorical devices must be invented for persuasion. But rhetoric will be thereby debased. In tyrannical states and extreme democracies, rhetoric is overtaken by "demagogery" and "flattery." Most polities will be between the ideal and its corruption, and, in general, rhetoric in the right hands is a force for good. Thus Aristotle left open the question of how much rhetoric may transcend expediency and self-interest to articulate fuller, richer, shared principles. He refused to divorce politics from morals and truth, but accepted the fact of divergence. By the same token, he believed that "artful" rhetorical skill is compatible with truth and morality. His primary purpose in writing about rhetoric was to describe the "civic art" of rhetoric in the best politics of the polity.[18]

But we cannot re-create an ideal polis in which Aristotle's art of rhetoric may be practiced.[19] Our civic life may not be conducive to his highest ideals. He regarded the quality of rhetoric as subordinate to and taking its character from the quality of the politics around it. It may be that our contemporary politics does not permit the rhetoric that we consider ideal. Debased rhetoric then contributes to its own corruption. However, awareness of the tension between ideal and real may show politicians how to move from partial justice toward fuller justice, how to broaden the inclusiveness of politics, and how to integrate competing claims on government. The challenge to political leadership is to recognize the kind of rhetoric that is "best" in different circumstances. Aristotle will not solve the problem of how to "teach reality" in the American polity. But perhaps he can give us some insights.

The good leader of a democratic polity must combine moral vision and practical intelligence. Advisers and policy experts cannot do this for a politician. He must invent a strategy for himself. Ronald Heifitz has called on leaders to bring citizens together in collaborative problem solving, which he calls "adaptive work."[20] The aim is to get citizens to work through policy problems by discussion, from which the leader may extract solutions acceptable to all. He gives the example of William Ruckleshaus, the head of the Environmental Protection Agency in the Reagan administration, who orchestrated a debate about pollution in the Pacific Northwest with the hope that dialogue would educate contending parties and bring them closer together. He did not give up his authority to make the final decision, but, as a result of the dialogue, his final decision was acceptable to all. This is perhaps a special kind of leadership that can work in a limited setting on one issue. But is adaptive work a realistic ideal for national politics and policy making? It occurs without being orchestrated when conflicting interests agree to bargains that have been brokered by politicians. But many conflicts are too intense or deep-seated for adaptive work to be effective. And it may be necessary for presidents to appeal to larger publics for the resolution of particular conflicts. Indeed, presidents may potentially have a comparative advantage over particular interests when they appeal to the general welfare. It may also be that the best they can do is win the agreement of their opponents that the steps they plan to take are at least legitimate first steps toward facing a problem. Heifitz regards Roosevelt as a past master at such leadership, and cites Johnson for similar leadership on civil rights. However, the Vietnam War was not amenable to adaptive work. The conflicts were too great. But perhaps this is an important point. National-security issues may not be conducive to adaptive work. But if action taken lacks public support in the long run, a policy will fail. Some kind of adaptive work must occur in the initial period of persuasion before action is final.

Heifitz identified the strategies of leadership that impede adaptive work: scapegoating, externalizing the enemy, using distracting issues or events, and jumping to premature conclusions. Certainly, Reagan's refusal to recognize his contribution to the escalating federal deficit, and his attempt to blame congressional Democrats, was a refusal to engage in adaptive work. He even rejected the suggestion of his own congressional leaders that a compromise be attempted.

Great personal self-confidence is required if presidents are to listen to and encourage views that conflict with theirs. They risk losing control of the process of policy making, but they may gain refined knowledge of the ingredients of potential solutions to both the politics and the policy problems. This stance is very different from the posture of presidents who present themselves as having the answers. Bruce Miroff contrasted Lincoln and FDR with presidents like Theodore Roosevelt and John Kennedy, who he sees as having engaged in macho, mock-heroic posturing that replaced action.[21] Whether one agrees with Miroff about TR and JFK is not important. What does matter is his clear understanding that leaders who listen and learn are more effective than those who rely on persona and image. We again see the close union of skill and character. It is important to remember that the highly manipulative leader will see life as a battleground and create situations in which standoffs occur. Daniel Goleman, an expert in "emotional intelligence," believes that effective leaders must fine-tune their performances, much as actors do, but must move beyond impression management to develop real strategies of persuasion.[22] It may be that persuasive actors must do this as well as they attempt to convey the authenticity of a range of human feelings. They draw on their experience and understanding of life, just as politicians must do.

F. G. Bailey has argued that political appeals that would be successful must rely on what Ibsen called "life's lie" to make life tolerable.[23] A social world without pretense would be too painful. For example, Americans must believe that equality of opportunity exists in our society, whether it does or not. We lie to ourselves. It would follow that practical politics accepts such illusions and dares not challenge them. Certainly, our personal and collective lives are permeated by illusions. Even creative adaptation to problems builds on partial illusion as a goad to action. But the very existence of political efforts to close the gap between the ideal and the real in American politics would seem to refute Bailey's belief that illusion is all.

Bailey has defined the task of a political leader as "a form of cultivating ignorance, of stopping doubts and stifling questions," requiring "the capacity to go beyond rationality, to operate by intuition, and to obliterate a scientific search for objective fact . . . [and] at the same time to convince the followers that the leader knows what he is doing." It is the "art" of "diseducation." Such talent for controlling followers requires "audacity" and is a skill that must be worked at. The central strategy is that of "exploiting cultures" by presenting a picture of reality that nullifies competing views. Popular anxiety is controlled by simplification rather than argument, and appeal to the heart and not the head. The audience is not being asked to verify, but to approve or disapprove.[24]

This description of necessary demagogy is consistent with the Aristotelian standards for good political rhetoric praised by Rorty and Oakeshott, both of whom do not see manipulation. The problem is that Bailey assumes an ideal rational world and does not understand that politics may validly encompass modes of thought other than rational discourse. For example, he writes, "The rationality of conflict is a flawed rationality, because the very complexity of the factors that must be taken into account require the frequent use of intuition, of playing a hunch, of trying one's luck."[25] But just so. Creative politicians must, by the nature of their work, exceed what is empirically known in their affirmations. But this can be done in an honest, open manner. Roosevelt's promise to experiment was much more honest rhetoric than Reagan's insistence on certainty. And the irony is that Reagan was not believed much of the time. His leadership rested on the engineering of economic recovery, not on adherence to his conservative principles.

According to Bailey, honest politicians are driven out of politics because they tell people what they do not want to hear. We can think of plenty of examples. Such failures discourage other politicians. Of course, politicians must evade hot issues until the moment seems propitious. But the starkness of the political drama at one time may be seen differently if the historical lens is widened. Victories of truth over illusion occur, but not at every moment in time. The ambition of idealistic politicians makes it so.

Contemporary democratic polities reveal a mutual disenchantment of publics and politicians. We do not fully understand the causes of the rift, but the remoteness of government, the distortions of politics by the media, and the intractability of many policy problems contribute to the distrust. We have a politics in which the political incentives of the main players do not, when taken in total, necessarily permit the resolution of conflict according to an understanding of a common good.

The breach of trust between politicians and citizens may reflect an implicit awareness that transactional politics lacks the resources, by itself, to foster the shared values and ideals of the commonweal. The healthiest politics, in the long run, is that of affirmation of the strongest ideals of the American polity. This is not achieved in a moment. But without such politics, the polity lacks vitality. American politics moves back and forth between pragmatism and transcendentalism, and each needs the other. Neither has indulged in the dark politics of hatred and prejudice, which has been a secondary theme throughout American history. The primary pattern is that of normal politics punctuated by periods of reform. And the current frustration with contemporary politics may stem from the desire for a period of reform without the understanding of what forms it should take. But this question can be resolved only through politics.

❖ ❖ ❖

ARISTOTLE AND MACHIAVELLI

Machiavelli invented the idea of the "worldly executive," who would direct government in response to the necessity of keeping the state strong and intact.[26] Virtue for Machiavelli was the faculty of foreseeing necessity, which is the dark side of "discernment." Acting from necessity may violate the normal morality of ordinary life in the interests of the state. Machiavelli's political science advises rulers how to do this. Even in a republic, the ruler controls the people as he leads them. Ambitious princes must be prudent, but prudence is cleverness.

Aristotle's ruler teaches that politics should be like friendship. The demagogue preaches illusion, and thereby weakens the state as the false myths are exposed by experience. The intelligent leader affirms the strengths of the state. Aristotle gives us an attainable polity and suggests countless ways in which it may be realistically improved. The challenge to a normative science of comparative politics is clear. Modern executives may learn from Aristotle that the political arts, at their best, will encourage "the better angels of our nature."

NOTES

Preface

1. My books on the presidency are *Presidential Leadership, Personality and Political Style* (New York: Macmillan, 1966); *The Power of the Modern Presidency* (New York: Knopf, 1974); *Presidents, Politics and Policy* (Baltimore: Johns Hopkins University Press, 1984), co-authored with Michael Nelson; and *Jimmy Carter as President: Leadership and the Politics of the Public Good* (Baton Rouge: Louisiana State University Press, 1988).

2. My work on political and administrative leadership includes *Leadership and Innovation: A Biographical Perspective on Entrepreneurs in Government,* with Jameson W. Doig and others (Baltimore: Johns Hopkins University Press, 1987); *Impossible Jobs in Public Management* (Lawrence: University Press of Kansas, 1988), with John Glidewell and others; and *Prisoners of Myth: The Leadership of the Tennessee Valley Authority, 1933–1990* (Princeton; N.J.: Princeton University Press, 1994).

3. Quoted in Quentin Bell, *Virginia Woolf: A Biography* (New York: Harcourt Brace Jovanovich, 1972), 172.

4. The idea of "teaching reality" as the most important thing that presidents do was expressed to me in private conversation by Richard Neustadt at a symposium in his honor held at the Woodrow Wilson Center, in Washington, D.C., June 1996.

5. Abraham Lincoln, first inaugural address, 4 March 1861, quoted in Benjamin P. Thomas, *Abraham Lincoln: a Biography* (New York: Knopf, 1952), 248.

CHAPTER 1
Power and Purpose

1. Abraham Lincoln, first inaugural address, 4 March 1861, quoted in Benjamin P. Thomas, *Abraham Lincoln: A Biography* (New York: Knopf, 1952), 248.

2. Alexander Hamilton, James Madison, and John Jay, *The Federalist: A Commentary on the Constitution of the United States* (New York: Modern Library, 1941), 337.

3. William Shakespeare, *Julius Caesar,* edited by Arthur Humphreys (Oxford: Clarendon Press, 1984).

4. Bernard Crick, *In Defense of Politics* (Baltimore: Penguin, 1964), 18.

5. Quoted in Arthur Schlesinger, Jr., *The Age of Roosevelt,* vol. 2, *The Coming of the New Deal* (Boston: Houghton Mifflin, 1959), 233.

6. Aristotle, *The Politics of Aristotle* (New York: Oxford University Press, 1958), 233.

7. Ibid., 41–42.

8. Ibid., 118.

9. Arlene W. Saxonhouse, *Fear of Diversity: The Birth of Political Science in Ancient Greek Thought* (Chicago: University of Chicago Press, 1992), 213–14; Bernard Yack, *The Problem of a Political Animal: Community, Justice, and Conflict in Aristotelian Political Thought* (Berkeley: University of California Press, 1993), 64–65.

10. Yack, *Problem of a Political Animal,* 18; Alasdair McIntyre, *Whose Justice? Whose Rationality?* (South Bend, Ind.: Notre Dame University Press, 1988), 93. McIntyre makes the point that Plato clearly differentiates the ideal form from real-life particularities, whereas Aristotle sees ideal forms in the particulars. In this sense, moral truths are always immanent in real-life existence for Aristotle. One discovers moral truth through social experience.

11. Stephen G. Salkever, *Finding the Mean: Theory and Practice in Aristotelian Political Philosophy* (Princeton, N.J.: Princeton University Press, 1991), 131.

12. Aristotle, *Politics,* 131.

13. Ibid., 114–15.

14. R. G. Mulgan, *Aristotle's Political Theory* (Oxford: Clarendon Press, 1977), 82–83.

15. Aristotle, *Politics,* 103–5.

16. Ibid., 124–26; Alasdair McIntyre, *After Virtue: A Study in Moral Theory* (Notre Dame, Ind.: University of Notre Dame Press, 1984), 159.

17. J. G. A. Pocock, *The Machiavellian Moment: Florentine Political Thought and the Atlantic Republican Tradition* (Princeton, N.J.: Princeton University Press, 1975), 72.

18. Aristotle, *Politics,* 115–18.

19. Ibid., 178.

20. Ibid., 180–81.

21. Pocock, *Machiavellian Moment*, 73.

22. Aristotle, *Politics*, 229; McIntyre, *Whose Justice?* 109.

23. Aristotle, *Politics*, 106.

24. Ibid., 147.

25. Ibid., 123; Aristotle, *The Ethics of Aristotle*, introduction by J. A. Smith (New York: Dutton, 1950), 278.

26. Aristotle, *Politics*, 155.

27. Aristotle, *Ethics*, 143–44.

28. Ibid., 153.

29. Ibid., 156.

30. Ibid., 274.

31. Aristotle, *Politics*, 232–33.

32. Ibid., 262.

33. Salkever, *Finding the Mean*, 131.

34. Ibid., 48.

35. Ibid., 8.

36. Ibid., 218.

37. Yack, *Problem of a Political Animal*, 135–37.

38. Pocock, *Machiavellian Moment*, 74–75.

39. Niccolò Machiavelli, *The Prince and the Discourses* (New York: Modern Library, 1950), 56–57.

40. Machiavelli, *Prince*, 27, 35, 38, 67, 69, 81.

41. Ibid., 91–94; Pocock, *Machiavellian Moment*, 25–26; Hannah Pitkin, *Fortune Is a Woman: Gender and Politics in the Thought of Niccolò Machiavelli* (Berkeley: University of California Press, 1984), 25–26.

42. Machiavelli, *Discourses*, 11.

43. Pocock, *Machiavellian Moment*, 212.

44. Ibid., 212–13. Of course, the Greek city-states also had citizen soldiers, but Aristotle was not an imperialist.

45. Machiavelli, *Discourses*, 146–48; Edward B. Portis, *Reconstructing the Classics: Political Theory from Plato to Marx* (Chatham, N.J.: Chatham House, 1994), 69–70.

46. Machiavelli, *Discourses*, 64–67; Portis, *Reconstructing the Classics*, 72.

47. Machiavelli, *Discourses*, 120.

48. Ibid., 260–63, 183–88.

49. Eugene Garvey, *Machiavelli and the History of Prudence* (Madison: University of Wisconsin Press, 1987), 1, 11.

50. Ibid., 13–16.

51. Pitkin, *Fortune Is a Woman*, 7–12.

52. Ibid., 286–87.

53. Harvey Mansfield, *Taming the Prince: The Ambivalence of Modern Executive Power* (New York: Free Press, 1989), 127.

54. Ibid., 129, 145.

55. Ibid., 285–86.

56. E. M. W. Tillyard, *Shakespeare's History Plays* (New York: Macmillan, 1946), 28–30.

57. Alan Bloom, with Harry Jaffa, *Shakespeare's Politics* (Chicago: University of Chicago Press, 1964), 9.

58. John Palmer, *The Political Characters of Shakespeare* (New York: Macmillan, 1948), ix.

59. Tillyard, *Shakespeare's History Plays*, 282.

60. Palmer, *Political Characters*, 247.

61. Tillyard, *Shakespeare's History Plays*, 258–59.

62. Kenneth Muir, introduction to William Shakespeare, *The Tragedy of King Richard the Second* (New York: Penguin, 1987), xxxii.

63. Shakespeare, *Richard II*, act 2, scene 1, 68.

64. Ibid., act 4, scene 1, 116.

65. Ibid., 117.

66. Ibid.

67. Ibid., act 5, scene 4, 147.

68. Derek Traversi, "From *Shakespeare from Richard II to Henry V*," in Shakespeare, *Richard II*, 236–37.

69. Palmer, *Political Characters*, 160.

70. Ibid.

71. William Shakespeare, *The History of Henry the Fourth*, Part 2 (New York: Pocket Books, 1976), act 4, scene 5, 102–3.

72. Tillyard, *Shakespeare's History Plays*, 266; Maynard Mack, introduction to William Shakespeare, *Henry IV*, Part 1 (New York: Penguin, 1987), xxv–xxvi.

73. Shakespeare, *Henry IV*, Part 1, act 1, scene 2, 50–51.

74. Palmer, *Political Characters*, 184–86.

75. Shakespeare, *Henry IV*, Part 2, act 4, scene 4, 92–93.

76. Shakespeare, *Henry IV*, Part 1, act 5, scene 4, 147–48.

77. Mack, introduction, xxxiv; Tillyard, *Shakespeare's History Plays*, 271.

78. Cleanth Brooks and Robert S. Heilman, "From *Understanding Drama*," in Shakespeare, *Henry IV*, Part 1, 268.

79. Robert Ornstein, "From *A Kingdom for a Stage*," in Shakespeare, *Henry IV*, Part 1, 259.

80. Mack, introduction, xxxv.

81. Shakespeare, *Henry IV*, Part 2, act 5, scene 5, 122–23.

82. Ibid., act 5, scene 2, 113.

83. Tillyard, *Shakespeare's History Plays,* 310–11.

84. Palmer, *Political Characters,* 221.

85. Ibid., 225–26.

86. Ibid., 228.

87. Ibid., 231.

88. William Shakespeare, *Henry V* (New York: New American Library, 1965), act 4, scene 1, 121.

89. Ibid., act 4, scene 3, 127.

90. Ibid., 126.

91. Tillyard, *Shakespeare's History Plays,* 295.

92. Shakespeare, *Henry V,* act 4, scene 1, 115.

93. Palmer, *Political Characters,* 246.

94. Honor Matthews, *Character and Symbol in Shakespeare's Plays* (Cambridge: Cambridge University Press, 1962), 54–56.

95. Ibid., 171.

96. Ibid., 162; Tillyard, *Shakespeare's History Plays,* 317.

97. F. G. Bailey, *Humbuggery and Manipulation: The Art of Leadership* (Ithaca, N.Y.: Cornell University Press, 1988), 4.

98. Gunnar Myrdal, *An American Dilemma: The Negro Problem in Modern Democracy* (New York: Harper, 1944).

99. Max Weber, "Politics as a Vocation," in *From Max Weber, Essays in Sociology,* edited by H. H. Gerth and C. Wright Mills (New York: Oxford University Press, 1958), 109.

100. Ibid., 115–17.

101. Garry Wills, *Lincoln at Gettysburg: The Words that Remade America* (New York: Simon and Schuster, 1992), 168.

102. Richard Hofstadter, *The American Political Tradition and the Men Who Made It* (New York: Vintage Books, 1948), 132.

103. William Safire, *Freedom* (New York: Doubleday, 1987), 620.

104. J. David Greenstone, *The Lincoln Persuasion: Remaking American Liberalism* (Princeton, N.J.: Princeton University Press, 1993), chaps. 9, 10.

105. Thomas, *Abraham Lincoln,* 497–98.

CHAPTER 2
Conceptions of Leadership

1. Woodrow Wilson, *Constitutional Government in the United States* (New York: Columbia University Press, 1908), 68–70.

2. Franklin Roosevelt, in *New York Times,* 13 November 1932, sec. 8, p. 1, quoted in Wilfred E. Binkley, *The Power of the Presidency: Problems of American Democracy* (Garden City N.Y.: Doubleday, Doran, 1937), 267.

3. Pendleton Herring, *Presidential Leadership: The Political Relations of Congress and the Executive* (New York: Rhineland, 1940).

4. Richard E. Neustadt, *Presidential Power and the Modern Presidents* (New York: Free Press, 1990). Part 1 of this edition is the book as first published in 1960, the version that is regarded as a classic.

5. Richard E. Neustadt, "What Did I Think I Was Doing?" *Presidential Research* 7, no. 2 (1985): 4.

6. James MacGregor Burns, *Leadership* (New York: Harper & Row, 1975), 390–91.

7. Ibid., 409.

8. Ibid., 34.

9. Ibid., 3, 389.

10. William H. Riker, "Political Science and Rational Choice," in *Perspectives on Positive Political Economy,* edited by James A. Alt and Kenneth A. Shepsle (New York: Cambridge University Press, 1990), 175.

11. William H. Riker, *The Art of Political Manipulation* (New Haven, Conn.: Yale University Press, 1986), chap. 2.

12. David M. Potter, *The Impending Crisis, 1846–1861* (New York: Harper & Row, Torch Books, 1976), 335–39.

13. William Shakespeare, *Henry IV,* Part 1 (New York: Penguin, 1987), act 3, scene 1, 98.

14. Stephen Skowronek, *The Politics Presidents Make: Leadership from John Adams to George Bush* (Cambridge, Mass.: Harvard University Press, Belknap Press, 1993), pt. 1.

15. Charles O. Jones, *The Presidency in a Separated System* (Washington DC: Brookings Institution, 1994); Mark A. Peterson, *Legislating Together: The White House and Capitol Hill from Eisenhower to Reagan* (Cambridge, Mass.: Harvard University Press, 1990).

16. Max Weber, "Politics as a Vocation," in *From Max Weber: Essays in Sociology,* edited by H. H. Gerth and C. Wright Mills (New York: Oxford University Press, 1958).

17. John Dewey, *Experience and Nature* (New York: Dover, 1958), chap. 1.

18. Aristotle, *The Ethics of Aristotle* (New York: Dutton, 1950), 27–28.

19. Burns, *Leadership,* 3.

20. Ibid., 42.

CHAPTER 3
Cultural Leadership

1. Gordon S. Wood, *The Creation of the American Republic 1776–1787* (Chapel Hill: University of North Carolina Press, 1969).

2. James Sterling Young, "On Nation Leading in America: Thinking About the Presidency, Political Culture, and the Culture of Nation in a Nation of Many Cultures" (Occasional Paper, Miller Center of Public Affairs, University of Virginia, Charlottesville, 1993). Young's idea of the "leadership regime" has very much informed the analysis that follows.

3. James MacGregor Burns, *Leadership* (New York: Harper & Row, 1975), 25–26; Young, "Nation Leading in America," 2.

4. Richard E. Neustadt, *Presidential Power and the Modern Presidents* (New York: Free Press, 1990), 154–55.

5. Dixon Wecter, *The Hero in America: A Chronicle of Hero-Worship* (New York: Scribner, 1941), 487.

6. H. Mark Roelofs, "The Prophetic President: Charisma in the American Political Tradition" (Manuscript, 1989).

7. Louis Hartz, *The Liberal Tradition in America: An Interpretation of American Political Thought Since the Revolution* (New York: Harcourt, Brace, 1955), 3–9.

8. Ibid., 62.

9. Richard J. Ellis, *American Political Cultures* (New York: Oxford University Press, 1993), 5, 7–8, 11–12, 15, 25, 28, 43, 59–60, 95.

10. Rogers M. Smith, "Beyond Tocqueville, Myrdal, and Hartz: The Multiple Traditions in America," *American Political Science Review* 87 (1993): 549–50.

11. Richard M. Merelman, *Making Something of Ourselves: On Culture and Politics in the United States* (Berkeley: University of California Press, 1984), 1–2.

12. Robert Bellah, Richard Madsen, William M. Sullivan, Ann Swidler, and Steven M. Tipton, *Habits of the Heart: Individualism and Commitment in American Life* (Berkeley: University of California Press, 1985), 256.

13. C. Wright Mills, *Power, Politics and People,* edited by Irving Louis Horowitz (New York: Oxford University Press, 1963), 191.

14. Michael Sandel, "The Political Theory of the Procedural Republic," in *The Power of Public Ideas,* edited by Robert Reich (Cambridge: Harvard University Press, 1990), 110–13.

15. Hadley Cantril and Lloyd Free, *The Political Beliefs of Americans: A Study of Public Opinion* (New Brunswick, N.J.: Rutgers University Press, 1967).

16. Stanley Feldman and John Zaller, "The Political Culture of Ambivalence: Ideological Responses to the Welfare State," *American Journal of Political Science* 36, no. 1 (1992): 268–72, 273–74, 281–82, 289–98.

17. Donald J. Devine, *The Political Culture of the United States: The Influence of Member Values on Regime Maintenance* (Boston: Little, Brown, 1972), 132, 261, 284–85.

18. Herbert McCloskey and John Zaller, *The American Ethos: Public Attitudes Towards Capitalism and Democracy* (Cambridge, Mass.: Harvard University Press, 1984), 287–88, 67–72, 80–82, 91–99, 114–15.

19. Arthur Schlesinger, "The Tides of National Politics," in *Paths to the Present* (New York: Macmillan, 1947), chap. 4.

20. Arthur Schlesinger, Jr., "The Cycles of American Politics," in *The Cycles of American History* (Boston: Houghton Mifflin, 1986), chap. 2.

21. David Resnick and Norman C. Thomas, "Cycling Through Politics" *Polity* 23, no. 1 (Fall 1990).

22. John Lewis Gaddis, *Strategies of Containment: A Critical Appraisal of Post-War American National Security Policy* (New York: Oxford University Press, 1982), 345–46.

23. Jameson Doig and Erwin C. Hargrove, *Leadership and Innovation: A Biographical Perspective on Entrepreneurs in Government* (Baltimore: Johns Hopkins University Press, 1986), chap. 1.

24. John W. Kingdon, *Agendas, Alternatives, and Public Policies* (Boston: Little, Brown, 1984), 155, 162–72.

25. John G. Geer, *From Tea Leaves to Opinion Polls: Politicians, Information, and Leadership* (New York: Columbia University Press, 1996), 180–181.

26. Frank R. Baumgartner and Bryan D. Jones, *Agendas and Instability in American Politics* (Chicago: University of Chicago Press, 1993), 13–16, 25–29, 237.

27. James A. Stimson, *Public Opinion in America: Moods, Cycles, and Springs* (Boulder, Colo.: Westview Press, 1991), 2–6, 17–23, 39, 46–47, 80–81, 110–13, 125, 248; Baumgartner and Jones, *Agendas and Instability*, 240–48.

28. Benjamin Page, *Choices and Echoes in Presidential Elections: Rational Man and Electoral Democracy* (Chicago: University of Chicago Press, 1978), 287–89, 353–57.

29. Samuel L. Popkin, *The Reasoning Voter: Communication and Persuasion in Presidential Campaigns* (Chicago: University of Chicago Press, 1991), 32–33, 42, 72–75, 96–101.

30. Page, *Choices and Echoes*, 363–65.

31. William G. Jacoby, "The Structure of Ideological Thinking in the

American Electorate," *American Journal of Political Science*, 39, no. 2 (1995): 314–23, 329–32.

32. William Schneider, "Democrats and Republicans, Liberals and Conservatives," in *Emerging Coalitions in American Politics*, edited by Seymour Martin Lipset (San Francisco: Institute for Contemporary Studies, 1978), chap. 8.

33. Feldman and Zaller, "Political Culture of Ambivalence," 272–83, 289–93.

34. McCloskey and Zaller, *American Ethos*, 291–93.

CHAPTER 4
Franklin D. Roosevelt

1. Frank Freidel, *Franklin D. Roosevelt: The Apprenticeship* (Boston: Little, Brown, 1952), 73.

2. Ibid., 65.

3. Quoted in Frances Perkins, *The Roosevelt I Knew* (New York: Viking Press, 1946), 21.

4. Quoted in Arthur M. Schlesinger, Jr., *The Crisis of the Old Order* (Boston: Houghton, Mifflin, 1957), 406.

5. Quoted in Ted Morgan, *FDR: A Biography* (New York: Simon and Schuster, 1985), 552.

6. Frank Freidel, *Franklin D. Roosevelt: A Rendezvous with Destiny* (Boston: Little, Brown, 1990), 87–88.

7. Perkins, *Roosevelt I Knew*, 153.

8. Samuel I. Rosenman, *Working with Roosevelt* (New York: Harper and Brothers, 1952), 122.

9. Quoted in Morgan, *FDR*, 530.

10. Philip Abbott, *The Exemplary President: Franklin D. Roosevelt and the American Political Tradition* (Amherst: University of Massachusetts Press, 1990), 13.

11. Robert Eden, "On the Origins of the Regime of Pragmatic Liberalism: John Dewey, Adolf A. Berle, and FDR's Commonwealth Club Address of 1932," *Studies in American Political Development* 7 (1993): 74–150.

12. Edgar E. Robinson, *They Voted for Roosevelt: The Presidential Vote, 1932–1944* (Palo Alto, Calif.: Stanford University Press, 1947), 19–20.

13. Quoted in Halford R. Ryan, *Franklin D. Roosevelt's Rhetorical Presidency* (New York: Greenwood Press, 1988), 86.

14. Freidel, *Roosevelt: Rendezvous with Destiny*, 92.

15. John Morton Blum, *The Progressive Presidents: Theodore Roosevelt,*

Woodrow Wilson, Franklin D. Roosevelt, and Lyndon B. Johnson (New York: Norton, 1980), 123.

16. Arthur M. Schlesinger, Jr., *The Coming of the New Deal* (Boston: Houghton Mifflin 1959), 527–32.

17. Freidel, *Roosevelt: Rendezvous with Destiny,* 145–46, 154.

18. Ibid., 150.

19. Ryan, *Roosevelt's Rhetorical Presidency,* 6, 15–23, 162.

20. Rosenman, *Working with Roosevelt,* 92.

21. John Gunther, *Roosevelt in Retrospect* (New York: Harper & Row, 1950), 4.

22. Elmer E. Cornwell, Jr., *Presidential Leadership of Public Opinion* (Bloomington: University of Indiana Press, 1965), chap. 6.

23. Perkins, *Roosevelt I Knew,* 297–98.

24. Cornwell, *Presidential Leadership,* 136.

25. James McGregor Burns, *Roosevelt: The Lion and the Fox* (New York: Harcourt, Brace, 1957), 267.

26. Rexford G. Tugwell, *The Democratic Roosevelt* (Garden City, N.Y.: Doubleday, 1957), 335–36.

27. Freidel, *Roosevelt: Rendezvous with Destiny,* 202–3, 205–6, 207.

28. Rexford Tugwell, *The Art of Politics as Practiced by Three Great Americans: Franklin Delano Roosevelt, Luis and Fiorello H. La Guardia* (Garden City, N.Y.: Doubleday, 1958), 203.

29. Freidel, *Roosevelt: Rendezvous with Destiny,* 225, 277.

30. Rosenman, *Working with Roosevelt,* 154–55.

31. Sidney M. Milkis, "FDR and the Transcendence of Partisan Politics," *Political Science Quarterly* 100 (1985): 487, 496.

32. Freidel, *Roosevelt: Rendezvous with Destiny,* 233, 252–56.

33. Rosenman, *Working with Roosevelt,* 54.

34. Blum, *Progressive Presidents,* 142–43.

35. Alonzo Hamby, *Liberalism and Its Challengers: From FDR to Bush* (New York: Oxford University Press, 1992), 36–43.

36. Freidel, *Roosevelt: Rendezvous with Destiny,* 263–64, 315–22, 333–34, 352; Rosenman, *Working with Roosevelt,* 166–68; Robert A. Devine, *The Reluctant Belligerent: American Entry into World War II,* 2nd ed. (New York: Knopf, 1979), 69; Robert Dallek, *Franklin D. Roosevelt and American Foreign Policy, 1932–1945* (New York: Oxford University Press, 1979), 95; Blum, *Progressive Presidents,* 146–47.

37. Dallek, *Roosevelt and Foreign Policy,* 249–50; Rosenman, *Working with Roosevelt,* 242; Divine, *Reluctant Belligerent,* 106; Freidel, *Roosevelt: Rendezvous with Destiny,* 357.

38. Divine, *Reluctant Belligerent*, 135–36.

39. Blum, *Progressive Presidents*, 148–49.

40. Divine, *Reluctant Belligerent*, 148–50.

41. Dallek, *Roosevelt and Foreign Policy*, 288–89.

42. Ryan, *Roosevelt's Rhetorical Presidency*, 158–59.

CHAPTER 5
Lyndon B. Johnson

1. Paul K. Conkin, *Big Daddy from the Pedernales: Lyndon Baines Johnson* (Boston: Twayne, 1986); Alonzo L. Hamby, *Liberalism and Its Challengers: From FDR to Bush* (New York: Oxford University Press, 1992); Doris Kearns, *Lyndon Johnson and the American Dream* (New York: Harper & Row, 1976).

2. William S. White, *Citadel: The Story of the U.S. Senate* (New York: Harper, 1957).

3. Conkin, *Big Daddy*, 134–35; Hamby, *Liberalism and Its Challengers*, 242–44; Kearns, *Johnson and American Dream*, 121–24.

4. Kearns, *Johnson and American Dream*, 117.

5. Conkin, *Big Daddy*, 139–42.

6. Quoted in Joseph A. Califano, *The Triumph and Tragedy of Lyndon Johnson: The White House Years* (New York: Simon and Schuster, 1991), 104.

7. Hamby, *Liberalism and Its Challengers*, 251–54.

8. Conkin, *Big Daddy*, 174.

9. John Morton Blum, *The Progressive Presidents: Theodore Roosevelt, Woodrow Wilson, Franklin D. Roosevelt, and Lyndon B. Johnson* (New York: WW Norton, 1980), 166–68; Kearns, *Johnson and American Dream*, 186–87.

10. Editorial, *Fortune*, 15 April 1964, quoted in Kearns, *Johnson and American Dream*, 187–88.

11. Kearns, *Johnson and American Dream*, 190–92; Conkin, *Big Daddy*, 215; David Culbert, "Johnson and the Media," in *The Johnson Years*, edited by Robert A. Devine (Lawrence: University Press of Kansas, 1987), 235–37.

12. Blum, *Progressive Presidents*, 167.

13. Conkin, *Big Daddy*, 188–89; Hamby, *Liberalism and Its Challengers*, 257–59.

14. Brian Van De Mark, *Into the Quagmire: Lyndon Johnson and the Escalation of the Vietnam War* (New York: Oxford University Press, 1991).

15. Wilbur Cohen, oral history, 2 March 1969, 2, 16–17, Lyndon Baines Johnson Library, University of Texas, Austin.

16. Robert C. Wood, oral history, 28 November 1969, 13, Lyndon Baines Johnson Library.

17. Walter Heller, in Erwin C. Hargrove and Samuel A. Morley, *The President and the Council of Economic Advisers: Interviews with the CEA Chairmen* (Boulder, Colo.: Westview Press, 1984), 172, 176–77.

18. Phillip Sam Hughes, oral history, 1 August 1974, 23, Lyndon Baines Johnson Library.

19. Joseph A. Califano, oral history, Lyndon Baines Johnson Library, 11 January 1973, 25.

20. Cohen, oral history, 1–4, 7, 15, 24–25.

21. Douglas Cater, oral history, 29 April 1969, 27, Lyndon Baines Johnson Library.

22. Hughes, oral history, 20; Califano, *Triumph and Tragedy,* 173.

23. Quoted in Califano, *Triumph and Tragedy,* 19.

24. Hamby, *Liberalism and Its Challengers,* 270; Conkin, *Big Daddy,* 56.

25. Stephen Skowronek, *The Politics Presidents Make: Leadership from John Adams to George Bush* (Cambridge, Mass.: Harvard University, Belknap Press, 1993), 327–28.

26. Conkin, *Big Daddy,* 213–14.

27. Hamby, *Liberalism and Its Challengers,* 260–61; Kearns, *Johnson and American Dream,* 307–08.

28. Blum, *Progressive Presidents,* 180–81.

29. Gardner Ackley, in Hargrove and Morley, *President and Council of Economic Advisers,* 250–51.

30. Blum, *Progressive Presidents,* 175–78.

31. Lyndon Johnson, telephone conversations with Robert McNamara, 20 February 1964, and J. William Fulbright, 2 March 1964, in *Taking Charge: The Johnson White House Tapes,* edited by Michael R. Bechloss (New York: Simon and Schuster, 1997), 248–50, 264.

32. Leslie H. Gelb, with Richard K. Betts, *The Irony of Vietnam: The System Worked* (Washington D.C.: Brookings Institution, 1979), 106–7, 144; Robert S. McNamara, with Brian Van De Mark, *In Retrospect: The Tragedy and Lessons of Vietnam* (New York: Random House, 1995), 113.

33. Gelb and Betts, *Irony of Vietnam,* 164.

34. McNamara, *In Retrospect,* 33–36, 49–50, 85, 101, 122–25, 156–58, 195.

35. Kearns, *Johnson and American Dream,* 258–59; Conkin, *Big Daddy,* 252.

36. McNamara, *In Retrospect,* 156–58, 188–89, 210, 261.

37. Blema S. Steinberg, *Shame and Humiliation: Presidential Decision Making on Vietnam* (Pittsburgh: University of Pittsburgh Press, 1996), chaps. 2, 3.

38. George C. Herring, "The War in Vietnam," in *Johnson Years,* edited by Devine, 39.

39. McNamara, *In Retrospect,* 175–76; Van De Mark, *Into the Quagmire,* 212–14; Conkin, *Big Daddy,* 243–44.

40. Califano, *Triumph and Tragedy,* 172–74.

41. Benjamin Page, *Choices and Echoes in Presidential Elections: Rational Man and Electoral Democracy* (Chicago: University of Chicago Press, 1978), 33–36.

42. Gelb and Betts, *Irony of Vietnam,* 172–73.

43. G. K. Chesterton, *Charles Dickens: The Last of the Great Men* (New York: Reader's Club, 1942), quoted in Wilson C. McWilliams, "Lyndon Johnson: The Last of the Great Presidents," in *Modern Presidents and the Presidency,* edited by Marc Landy (Lexington, Mass.: Heath, 1985), 6.

44. Cohen, oral history, 13–15.

45. Hamby, *Liberalism and Its Challengers,* 260–62; Kearns, *Johnson and American Dream,* 217; Conkin, *Big Daddy,* 221.

46. Califano, *Triumph and Tragedy,* 25–27.

CHAPTER 6
Ronald Reagan

1. Lou Cannon, *President Reagan, the Role of a Lifetime* (New York: Simon and Schuster, 1991), 210; Haynes Johnson, *Sleepwalking Through History: America in the Reagan Years* (New York: Norton, 1991), 43–44; Robert Dallek, *Ronald Reagan: The Politics of Symbolism* (Cambridge, Mass.: Harvard University Press, 1984), 13–14; Garry Wills, *Reagan's America* (New York: Penguin 1988), 28, 34.

2. Wills, *Reagan's America,* 62–63; Dallek, *Reagan,* 8–9, 18.

3. Wills, *Reagan's America,* 130, 141–42, 151–58.

4. Alonzo L. Hamby, *Liberalism and Its Challengers: From FDR to Bush* (New York: Oxford University Press, 1992), 343; Dallek, *Reagan,* 7–8, 19–20; Wills, *Reagan's America,* 210.

5. Wills, *Reagan's America,* 144–47.

6. Dallek, *Reagan,* 25–26; Wills, *Reagan's America,* 337–38.

7. Wills, *Reagan's America,* 340–41, 346.

8. Ibid., 351–54; Dallek, *Reagan,* 37.

9. Hamby, *Liberalism and Its Challengers,* 349–50; Wills, *Reagan's America,* 369, 372; Dallek, *Reagan,* 50; Cannon, *President Reagan,* 114.

10. Wills, *Reagan's America,* 365; Dallek, *Reagan,* 52, 56–57.

11. Michael Deaver, with Mickey Herskowitz, *Behind the Scenes* (New York: Morrow, 1987), 73; Cannon, *President Reagan,* 116.

12. Deaver, *Behind the Scenes*, 40, 73; Cannon, *President Reagan*, 217–20, 226; Wills, *Reagan's America*, 43; Johnson, *Sleepwalking Through History*, 41–42.

13. Hamby, *Liberalism and Its Challengers*, 353–54, 356–60; Wills, *Reagan's America*, 361; Johnson, *Sleepwalking Through History*, 130.

14. Wills, *Reagan's America*, 429; Dallek, *Reagan*, 60; Hamby, *Liberalism and Its Challengers*, 361; Paul Allen Beck, "Incomplete Realignment: The Reagan Legacy for Parties and Elections," in The Reagan Legacy: Promise and Performance, edited by Charles Jones (Chatham, N.J.: Chatham House, 1988), 160–68; Amos Kiewe and Davis W. Houck, *A Shining City on a Hill: Ronald Reagan's Economic Rhetoric* (New York: Praeger, 1991), 136; James Ceaser, "The Reagan Presidency and American Public Opinion," in *Reagan Legacy*, edited by Jones, 178; Kurt Ritter and David Henry, *Ronald Reagan: The Great Communicator* (New York: Greenwood Press, 1992), 139.

15. Cannon, *President Reagan*, 71–72, 107–8, 111; Ritter and Henry, *Reagan: Great Communicator*, 141.

16. Mark A. Peterson, *Legislating Together: The White House and Capitol Hill from Eisenhower to Reagan* (Cambridge, Mass.: Harvard University Press, 1990), 161; Johnson, *Sleepwalking Through History*, 104; Cannon, *President Reagan*, 240.

17. Robert Shogun, *The Riddle of Power: Presidential Leadership from Truman to Bush* (New York: Penguin 1992), 248–49; Cannon, *President Reagan*, 93, 154, 238–39, 246, 255–56, 260–62, 287.

18. Peterson, *Legislating Together*, 269; Lawrence I. Barrett, *Gambling with History: Reagan in the White House* (New York: Penguin, 1984), 12; Stephen Skowronek, *The Politics Presidents Make: Leadership from John Adams to George Bush* (Cambridge, Mass.: Harvard University Press, Belknap Press, 1993), 424–25.

19. Wills, *Reagan's America*, 438; Dennis Florig, *The Power of Presidential Ideologies* (New York: Praeger, 1992), 197.

20. Cannon, *President Reagan*, 233, 269, 271, 274; Dallek, *Reagan*, 109–10, 111; Hamby, *Liberalism and Its Challengers*, 368–69; Skowronek, *Politics Presidents Make*, 426–27.

21. Dallek, *Reagan*, 118–19; Wills, *Reagan's America*, 437.

22. Cannon, *President Reagan*, 258, 829–30; Peterson, *Legislating Together*, 265–66; Aaron Wildavsky, "President Reagan as a Political Strategist," in *Reagan Legacy*, edited by Jones, 290–94.

23. Skowronek, *Politics Presidents Make*, 417–21; Peterson, *Legislating Together*, 261.

24. Hamby, *Liberalism and Its Challengers*, 387–88; Cannon, *President Rea-

gan, 515; Paul Peterson and Mark Rom, "Lower Taxes, More Spending, and Budget Deficits," in *Reagan Legacy*, edited by Jones, 236–37.

25. M. Stephen Weatherford and Lorraine M. McDonell, "Ideology and Economic Policy," in *Looking Back on the Reagan Presidency*, edited by Larry Berman (Baltimore: Johns Hopkins University Press, 1990), 141–43, 149–50.

26. Cannon, *President Reagan*, 252, 275–79, 307, 516–17; Johnson, *Sleepwalking Through History*, 391–93; Isabel Sawhill, "Overview," in *The Reagan Record*, edited by John L. Palmer and Isabel Sawhill (Cambridge, Mall.: Ballinger, 1984), 97; Herbert Stein, *Presidential Economics: The Making of Economic Policy from Roosevelt to Clinton* (Washington, D.C.: American Enterprise Institute, 1994), chap. 9.

27. Wills, *Reagan's America*, 233.

28. Fred I. Greenstein, "Ronald Reagan, Mikhail Gorbachev, and the End of the Cold War: What Difference Did They Make?" in *Witness to the End of the Cold War*, edited by William C. Wohlforth (Baltimore: Johns Hopkins University Press, 1996), 211, 217–18.

29. I. M. Destler, "Reagan and the World: An Awesome Stubbornness," in *Reagan Legacy*, edited by Jones, 242, 253.

30. Greenstein, "Ronald Reagan," 211–15.

31. Cannon, *President Reagan*, chap. 14.

32. *The Tower Commission Report: The Full Text of the President's Special Review Board* (New York: Bantam and Times Books, 1987), 63–64.

33. Cannon, *President Reagan*, 12, 41, 495; Robert E. Denton, Jr., *The Primetime Presidency of Ronald Reagan: The Era of the Television Presidency* (New York: Praeger, 1988), 66.

34. Ritter and Henry, Reagan: The Great Communicator, 116.

35. William K. Muir, Jr., *The Bully Pulpit: The Presidential Leadership of Ronald Reagan* (San Francisco: Center for Self-Governance of the Institute for Contemporary Studies, 1992), 13, 113.

36. This section on Reagan's rhetoric owes much to Hugh Heclo, "Reaganism and the Search for a Public Philosophy," in *Perspective on the Reagan Years*, edited by John L. Palmer, (Washington, D.C.: Urban Institute Press, 1986), 31–63.

37. Howard Gardner, *Frames of Mind: The Theory of Multiple Intelligence* (New York: Basic Books, 1983); Cannon, President Reagan, 132–33, 137–39.

38. Quoted in Cannon, *President Reagan*, 133.

39. Murray Edelman, *Political Language: Words that Succeed and Policies that Fail* (New York: Academic Press, 1977).

CHAPTER 7
Leadership of the Polity

1. Sidney Hook, *The Hero in History: A Study in Limitation and Possibility* (New York: Day, 1943).

2. Philip G. Cerny, "The Process of Personal Leadership: The Case of Charles de Gaulle," *International Political Science Review* 9, no. 2 (1988): 131–42. Cerny describes this kind of leadership as "catalytic."

3. Harold D. Lasswell, *Psychopathology and Politics* (Chicago: University of Chicago Press, 1930); Lasswell, *Power and Personality* (New York: Norton, 1948). The idea of "political man" dates from 1930, and the concept of "democratic character" was added in 1948.

4. James David Barber, *The Presidential Character* (Englewood Cliffs, N.J.: Prentice-Hall, 1985).

5. George E. Vaillant, *The Wisdom of the Ego* (Cambridge, Mass.: Harvard University Press, 1993), 2, 7, 17, 29, 35–38, 45–59, 66–75.

6. Ibid., 107.

7. Stanley A. Renshon, *The Psychological Assessment of Presidential Candidates* (New York: New York University Press, 1996).

8. Ibid., 89.

9. Jeffrey K. Tulis, *The Rhetorical Presidency* (Princeton: Princeton University Press, 1987), 161–72.

10. The best contemporary statement is Michael Sandel, *Democracy's Discontent: America in Search of a Public Philosophy* (Cambridge, Mass.: Harvard University Press, 1996).

11. Seymour Martin Lipset, *American Exceptionalism: A Double-Edged Sword* (New York: Norton, 1996), 19.

12. Ibid., 275.

13. Robert H. Wiebe, *Self-Rule: A Cultural History of American Democracy* (Chicago: University of Chicago Press, 1995), 243–65.

14. John Zaller, *The Nature and Origin of Mass Opinion* (New York: Cambridge University Press, 1992).

15. Richard Rorty, *Contingency, Irony, and Solidarity* (Cambridge: Cambridge University Press, 1989), xvi.

16. Michael Oakeshott, *Rationalism in Politics and Other Essays* (Indianapolis: Liberty Press, 1991), 78–79.

17. Aristotle, *The Rhetoric and Poetics of Aristotle* (New York: McGraw-Hill, 1984).

18. C. D. C. Reeve, "Philosophy, Politics, and Rhetoric in Aristotle," in *Essays on Aristotle's Rhetoric,* edited by Amelie Oksenberg Rorty (Berkeley: University of California Press, 1996), 191–205.

19. Eugene Garver, *Aristotle's Rhetoric: An Art of Character* (Chicago: University of Chicago Press, 1994).

20. Ronald A. Heifitz, *Leadership Without Easy Answers* (Cambridge, Mass.: Harvard University Press, Belknap Press, 1994).

21. Bruce Miroff, *Icons of Democracy: American Heroes, Aristocrats, Dissenters, and Democrats* (New York: Basic Books, 1993).

22. Daniel Goleman, *Emotional Intelligence* (New York: Bantam Books, 1995).

23. F. G. Bailey, *Humbuggery and Manipulation: The Art of Leadership* (Ithaca, N.Y.: Cornell University Press, 1988), 175.

24. Ibid., 4.

25. Ibid., 158.

26. Harvey C. Mansfield, *Taming the Prince: The Ambivalence of Modern Executive* Power (New York: Free Press, 1989), chap. 11.

INDEX

❖   ❖   ❖

Index

and conservative acceptance of
  leadership regime, 50
in consolidation sequence, 62
as consolidator, 64
North, Oliver, 151
NRA. *See* National Recovery
  Administration

Oakeshott, Michael, 185, 189
Oligarchy, 3, 6
Orwell, George, 19

Page, Benjamin, 73
Passion, 22
Patriotism, 45, 139
Patronage, 89, 90
Pensions, 88, 89, 93
People
  as represented by institutions,
    49
  as sovereign, 49
Pericles, 184
Perkins, Frances, 79, 94
Perot, Ross, 184
Personal responsibility, 183
Persuasion, 26–27, 28, 32, 34,
    35–36, 47, 48, 107, 153, 156,
    161, 162, 173, 177, 186, 189
  and reality, 173
Pitkin, Hannah, 12
Planters, 54
Plato, 4
Plausibility, 175
Pluralist polity, 25
Pluralist society, 29, 39, 53, 81, 116
Pocock, J. G. A., 6
Poindexter, John, 151
Policy
  and citizen discussion, 187–88
  coalitions, 63

constraints on, 61, 83
credibility, 124, 125, 128
domestic, 63, 64, 83, 86
entrepreneurs, 68, 110
and historical context, 169–70
innovation, 25, 70, 87
and political culture, 182
and public opinion, 68–69, 71,
    72
sequence change factors, 64–66
sequences, 61–67
See also under Politics
Polis, 4–7
Political action, 28
  concepts, 25
  context, 37
  limits of, 61
  realist, 41, 46
  on social and economic prob-
    lems, 64
Political culture
  and American dream, 53, 93
  blind spots/traps, 22, 45–46, 47,
    83, 175–76
  characteristics, 39, 61, 173, 183
    (*see also* Egalitarianism;
    Hierarchy; Individualism)
  and empowerment of president,
    51
  and inequalities, 55
  and institutional authority,
    50–51, 56, 57
  and leadership, 22, 23, 39, 40,
    41, 49–50
  limits, 182, 183
  prophetic tradition, 51–52
  and reform leadership, 165
  tensions, 57
  See also Leadership, cultural;
    Values